The Valencia Tragedy

Michael C. Neitzel

363.123097112 Nei

Neitzel, M.
The Valencia tragedy.

PRICE: $11.95 (3559/go   )

PHOTO CREDITS

Author: 28 (bottom), 105 (bottom); B.C. Archives and Records Service: 9, 39, 46, 53 (bottom), 55 (top), 56, 72 (bottom), 76 (bottom), 84, 91 (top), 98 (top), 105 (top); Maritime Museum of B. C.: 55 (bottom); Parks Canada: Outside Front Cover; Puget Sound Maritime Historical Society: 18-19, 63, 65, 67, 69 (bottom); Seattle Public Library: 19 (inset), 28, 32 (bottom), 42, 53, (top), 69 (top), 72 (top), 76 (top), 82, 107, 109; University of Washington: 12-13; Vancouver Public Library: 91 (bottom).

Copyright © 1995   Michael C. Neitzel

Canadian Cataloguing in Publication Data

Neitzel, Michael C., 1945 –
   The Valencia tragedy

   Includes bibliographical references and index.
   ISBN 1-895811-36-8

   1. Valencia (Steamship) 2. Shipwrecks – British Columbia –
Vancouver Island. I. Title.
FC3820.S5N44 1995   363.12'3'097112   C95-910055-5
F1089.V3N44 1995

No part of this publication may be reproduced, stored in a retrieval system, or transmitted in any form or by any means, electronic, mechanical, photocopying, recording or otherwise, without the prior permission of Heritage House Publishing Company Ltd.

First Edition – 1995

HERITAGE HOUSE PUBLISHING COMPANY LTD.
Unit #8, 17921 55th Ave., Surrey, B. C. V3S 6C4

Printed in Canada

ACKNOWLEDGEMENTS

I would like to thank my publisher and editor, Art Downs, for taking me on as a first-time author, and for his patience, valuable criticism, and good humour with which he guided me through my first book publication. I would also like to thank Leonard G. McCann, Curator of Maritime History at the Vancouver Maritime Museum, for never getting tired of my phone calls, and for pointing me in the right direction when my research got bogged down; Barry Campbell, Head Warden at Pacific Rim National Park, for reading the first draft and for his suggestions and corrections; Michael Paris, photographer and member of the Underwater Archaeological Society, for helping me with contacts when I needed them, and John MacFarlane for sharing with me the story of the *Valencia's* lifeboat No. 5. And last, but not least, I thank my family for their understanding, tolerance, and encouragement in the pursuit of my dreams, even if they often are not theirs as well.

THE AUTHOR

After returning home to Coquitlam from a 2 1/2-year-long sailing voyage with his family to the South Pacific and Australia, Michael re-discovered his love for writing and his interest in local maritime history. He has published many articles on sailing and the sea in magazines here and in Australia and has written other books, including one about their sailing adventure. A free spirit and adventurer at heart, Michael is most comfortable on their sailing ketch *Southern Cross*, planning his next ocean voyage. He is presently working on a screenplay about the *Valencia* tragedy, which he hopes will one day become a major motion picture.

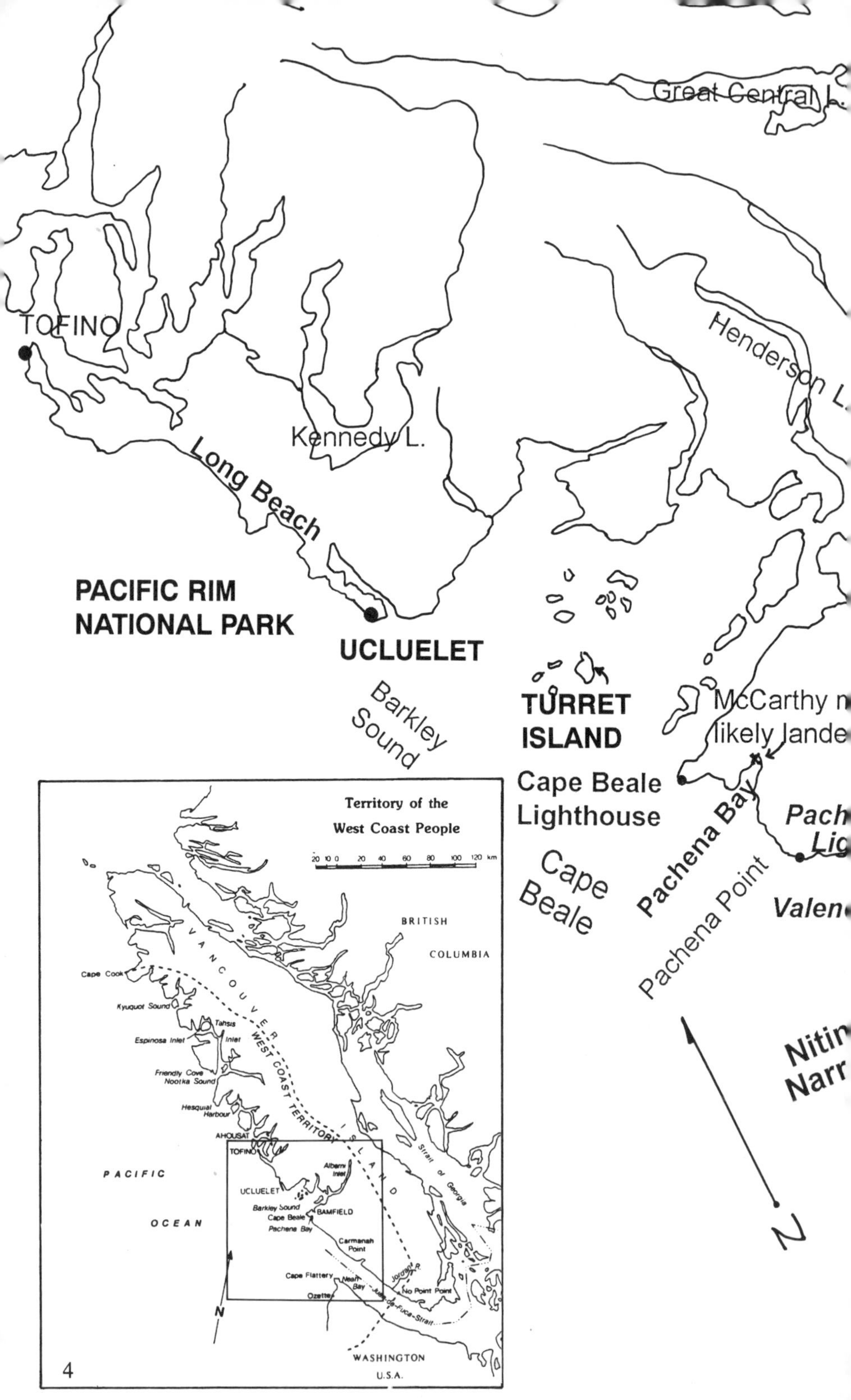
Great Central L.
TOFINO
Kennedy L.
Henderson L.
Long Beach
PACIFIC RIM
NATIONAL PARK
UCLUELET
Barkley
Sound
TURRET
ISLAND
McCarthy n
likely lande
Cape Beale
Lighthouse
Cape
Beale
Pachena Bay
Pachena Point
Pach
Lig
Valen
Nitin
Narr
N
Territory of the
West Coast People
20 10 0 20 40 60 80 100 120 km
BRITISH
COLUMBIA
VANCOUVER
ISLAND
WEST COAST TERRITORY
Cape Cook
Kyuquot Sound
Tahsis
Inlet
Espinosa Inlet
Friendly Cove
Nootka Sound
Hesquiat
Harbour
AHOUSAT
TOFINO
Alberni
Inlet
UCLUELET
Barkley Sound
Cape Beale
BAMFIELD
Pachena Bay
Carmanah
Point
Strait of Georgia
PACIFIC
OCEAN
Cape Flattery
Neah
Bay
Jordan R.
No Point Point
Ozette
Juan-de-Fuca-Strait
WASHINGTON
U.S.A.
N

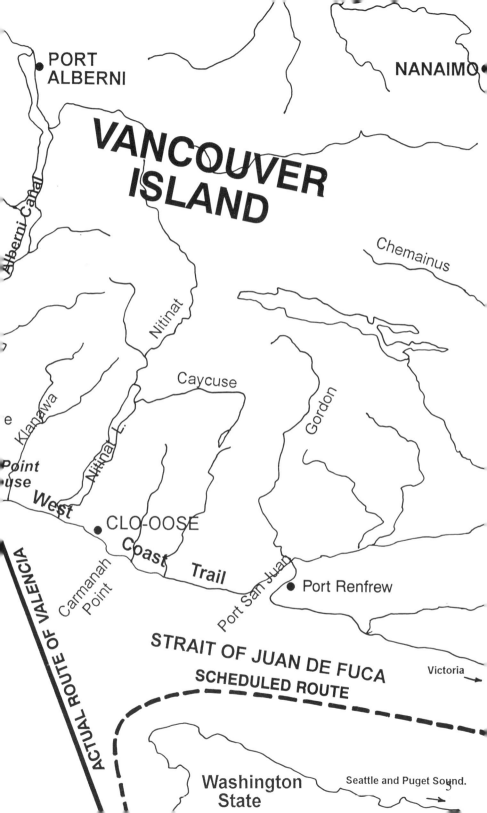

CONTENTS

Graveyard of the Pacific

It is always difficult to reconstruct an event like the tragedy of the *Valencia*. One has to rely on whatever testimony is available from survivors and eyewitnesses, and piece it together as best as possible. Because all those involved are dead, the information can only be second-hand. The result is that someone has already intertwined personal feelings, prejudices, interpretations and assumptions with the facts.

Reports by survivors of the wreck of the *Valencia* were the most valuable. Although eye witnesses often differed in their statements of the same event, I have used their testimony when I felt that it would make clearer to the reader and easier to understand what passengers and crew endured during the fateful last hours.

Some of the surviving passengers and crew were recent immigrants, and their English was not good. Others spoke crude English learned aboard ship, and that often was not so good either. But their description of the disaster in its intensity and the reflection of their personal feelings is deeply touching.

I recently visited the *Valencia's* grave off Pachena Point near the entrance to Barkley Sound on the west coast of Vancouver Island. It was a clear November day. A strong wind blew off the ocean, but it was a warm wind for the time of year. Warm and moist, bringing with it small droplets from the sea, a contrast to the big green ocean swells exploding on the rocky shore below. Over my left shoulder I could see the house of the lighthouse keeper and the old wooden tower of the lighthouse itself at Pachena Point. This structure is the last of the original wooden lighthouses on the west coast of Vancouver Island. The giant dioptric lens which concentrates the light turned slowly, at regular intervals sending out its piercing beam 24 hours a day.

To my left and only about 25 miles away, I could see the light on Tatoosh Island, marking Cape Flattery on the

Washington side of the Strait of Juan de Fuca. To my right, the rocky coast stretched on and on in the mist of early morning, disappearing in the far distance in the haze created by the pounding sea. Spray was flung upward into the silent trees, 100 feet above the water. This was still a remote and lonely coast, so wild and yet immensely beautiful.

Just below me I could see a big rock almost submerged in the sea. Between swells it would rise out of the green water, exposing its jagged edges, only to disappear from view a few seconds later under the onslaught of yet another big wave. As the swell receded the water ran off its surface like one endless waterfall, exposing a row of kelp. It looked like the skeleton of a ship, a reminder of the astonishing fact that some 300 vessels have been wrecked along this lonely stretch of coastline.

After spending several years sailing with my family on our small yacht through the paradise of the South Pacific Islands and Australia, I became interested in the waters around the coast of my British Columbia home. I had heard about "The Graveyard of the Pacific," a name given to the southwest coast of Vancouver Island along a short 35 miles of coastline between Port Renfrew and Cape Beale which marks the entrance to Barkley Sound.

In the early 1900s British Columbia had long been neglected by the Government in Ottawa – many people say that nearly a century later there has been no change – and few lights lit up this bleak expanse of coast. Although mariners from both sides of the border begged the Canadian Government to light up the west coast of Vancouver Island, their desperate cry for help was ignored year after year.

Few places in the world have such a record of marine casualties as this stretch of bleak and desolate capes and cliffs. This treacherous coast, which would soon claim the *Valencia,* had seen the destruction of 56 vessels with the loss of 711 lives in the 40 years before 1906.

In those days sailors navigated by a system still used today -- but only as a backup. It is called dead reckoning. A "patent log" – a device looking very much like an elongated propeller – was towed behind the ship and registered distance on a set of gauges mounted on the taffrail, hence the name "taffrail log." By calculating the time between readings and the magnetic course steered, an amazingly accurate estimation of

In the 40-year period prior to the *Valencia* disaster, 56 vessels were wrecked in the Graveyard of the Pacific with the loss of over 700 lives. Included was HMS *Condor,* above, a seaworthy British warship that disappeared with all 80 on board.

The worst disaster was the steamship *Pacific,* below, which collided with the *Orpheus* on the night of November 4, 1875. The official death toll was given as some 260, although many estimates put it at over 400. What is known is that only two survived. Next day the *Orpheus* struck the rocky shore near Cape Beale and was a total loss.

the ship's position could be made. There are problems, however, with this form of navigation. The taffrail log can only measure the distance travelled through the water, not over the seabed or in relation to fixed points of land. Compounding this problem is the Davidson Current which sweeps northward along the North American continent during the winter.

This current varies in strength in accordance with prevailing winds, and is very difficult to estimate exactly. During the frequent southerly gales the speed of the current is much increased. The current, combined with the often foggy and stormy weather, frequently caused unlucky mariners to overshoot the entrance to Juan de Fuca Strait. The consequence was that they were driven onto the rocky, desolate and uninhabited Vancouver Island coast. Here their ships were soon pounded to pieces. The sea had no mercy.

Sailing ships had no chance of getting off the rocks against a southerly gale. Steamships hardly fared any better, although some managed to back off and limp into Victoria Harbour with tales of terror. Quite often the first knowledge of imminent disaster came when the seaman who was sounding with the lead yelled: "Thirty fathoms!" and the lookout warned: "I can see breakers ahead!"

The captain would immediately try to reverse the ship, or drop anchor to try and stop his vessel. But the relentless power of the Pacific Ocean, driven by wind with no obstruction for almost 5,000 miles to the west, soon parted chains and ropes. One hundred-foot, wave-lashed cliffs would face the wrecked seamen. Even if they reached shore, they were mercilessly tossed by massive breakers onto the barnacle-covered rocks and boulders. Few survived.

All of these hundreds of wrecks were tragedies for those on board. None, however, before or since, equalled the terrible nightmare endured by those on the *S.S. Valencia*. She was wrecked near Pachena Point on the blustery night of January 22, 1906. Over 100 people, many of them women and children, lost their lives. The sinking was the most appalling display of bad luck, incompetence, negligence and lack of compassion for the victims in recorded Canadian maritime history.

CHAPTER ONE

"My God! Where Are We?"

The year was 1906. Theodore Roosevelt was in his second term as U.S. president, and the Prime Minister of the Dominion of Canada since 1896 was Sir Wilfrid Laurier. The population of the United States was 85 million, that of Canada just over 6 million, and the year before Alberta and Saskatchewan had been declared the newest provinces of Canada.

The production of automobiles in the United States reached 25,000 in 1905, and the famous Wright Brothers improved their flying machine of 1903 to the point where they could fly a full circle of 24.5 miles in 38 minutes. U.S. inventor Lee de Forest had developed a three-electrode vacuum tube amplifier that would greatly improve radio and wireless transmissions and save thousands of lives at sea. In 1906, a single family home, of beautiful Victorian design, not much different from the large urban home of today, sold in Victoria for $3,700.

Also in 1906, a beautiful sunny January 20, the steamer *Valencia* was tied up at the Embarcadero in San Francisco, getting ready for her trip north to Victoria and Seattle. The calls of the gulls mixed with the clatter from the *Valencia's* cranes, lifting the last pieces of cargo on board. Once in a while the blast of a steam whistle could be heard above the general commotion. Some passengers had climbed the ratlines on the forward mast to have a better view of the busy scene below.

Family and friends stood on the dock, waving and smiling to those already on board. Most men wore bowler hats or caps, and were dressed in dark suits, vests, and bow-ties for the occasion. The women wore fancy long dresses, and hats adorned with artificial flowers. The scent of the ocean mixed with the smells of creosote and tar, and the scene was charged with excitement and vitality. San Francisco Bay was covered with small whitecaps, and the Pacific Ocean beyond the Golden Gate glittered in the morning sunlight. The steamer blew her whistle three times, a sign of imminent departure.

The *Valencia* ready to leave San Francisco for Nome, Alaska, in 1905. A few months later the embarkation scene was repeated when she left for Victoria and Seattle.

Some wiped tears from their eyes as loved ones departed. The cook had come out on deck, and was leaning on the railing, smoking a cigarette. He surveyed the scene. He had already survived four shipwrecks and had an uneasy feeling. But there was no reason to feel apprehensive, he told himself. It was a fine day, the trip north was routine, and should not take longer than three or four days. Still, somehow he wished he were among those standing on the dock rather than on the *Valencia*. He sighed, threw the cigarette butt over the side and turned back towards the galley. It was time to prepare the evening meal. With a last look at the blue sky, he opened the door and stepped back inside.

The *Valencia* carried some 104 adult travellers in first and second class, including 17 women and small children, as well as 65 officers and crew. The exact number of passengers is unknown because many were never found, and many others unrecognizable in death, robbed of their human features and the dignity of a proper burial by the fury of the sea.

She was an iron, single-screw steamer with three decks and gross tonnage of just under 1,600. She was not fitted with a double bottom, and her hull construction was primitive. But she was a pretty ship, her black hull contrasted with her white upper decks, while her slanted single funnel and masts gave her a look of speed and determination. Built in 1882 at Philadelphia, she was 253 feet long and 34 wide. She was first operated under the flag of the Red Star Line, serving between New York and Central America. During the Spanish-American war in 1898 she operated as a government transport between San Francisco and Manila. She had subsequently been in service to Nome and Valdez in Alaska, and on California routes.

She arrived on the west coast late in 1898, owned by the Pacific Coast Company. She was, however, operated by the Pacific Coast Steamship Company, a subsidiary to the former who had purchased her for $150,000. The company had a poor safety record with disastrous consequences. On January 2, 1902, the steamship *Walla* under the command of Captain Hall was rammed by the French bark *Max* and sank off Cape Mendocino. Many lives were lost.

In another incident only two years later, the *Queen City* under Captain Cousins, who will play a major role in the account of the *Valencia* tragedy, caught fire at sea. Fourteen lives were lost.

On November 27, 1904, the steamer *Mainlander* sank after being rammed by the tug *Sea Lion*. Miraculously, no lives were lost.

Another company mishap would result in tragedy for many of those waving goodbye from the *Valencia*. She was not really supposed to undertake this voyage. The regular vessel for this run north to Juan de Fuca Strait was the *City of Pueblo*. But she had narrowly escaped disaster when she ran aground on the Columbia Bar and was currently under repair. The *Valencia* took her place. She, also, had not been a lucky ship.

On her last trip north to Nome, Alaska, in the fall of the previous year, she ran into a storm during which a portion of her cargo was lost overboard. Soon after, she ran aground while attempting to reach St. Michaels, Alaska. Her captain was Oscar Marcus Johnson, now destined to run her on the rocks for the last time near Pachena Point.

Among the crew there was a general feeling of uneasiness, unusual among the happy-go-lucky mariners. Seamen are traditionally suspicious, and when they heard that a black cat had come aboard in St. Michaels, they believed that some disaster awaited the ship. There had been other predictions of doom. There was the story of a wandering gypsy who had forecast approaching disaster, and had told the wife of the fourth officer that the ship would be wrecked. Then there was the cook who had already survived four wrecks. Just after the *Valencia* struck, he was supposed to have said:

"I knew it! I have known it all along that she was doomed!"

The *Valencia* was licensed to carry 286 passengers. She had three cargo holds, and carried a wide assortment of goods, from 60,000 pounds of beans for the Northwest Territories to 8 cases of metal polish for Suva, Fiji. She had four watertight metal bulkheads, two boilers, with six furnaces altogether, and was allowed a steam pressure of 100 pounds. Her last annual inspection was on April 27, 1905, in Seattle. In November 1905, she was reinspected, and on January 3, 1906, was again specially reinspected at San Francisco. These inspections were to become a controversial subject.

She was equipped with six lifeboats and one work boat, which was carried swung out on davits whenever at sea for emergency use. The lifeboats and the working boat had a capacity of 181 people. She also carried three liferafts, with a capacity of 44. Two of these rafts were made of tule, better known as "cattail," to provide floatation. This material would come under severe scrutiny and criticism during the investigation following the disaster. As well she carried 368 life preservers, 315 of which also were of tule, and the rest cork.

Four anchors with 90 fathoms of chain (540 feet) for each and a Lyle line-firing gun with 1,500 feet of line were also part of her equipment. (A Lyle gun is used to fire a thin rope up to 1,000 feet. This thin line can then be used to pull the much heavier main line. On the *Valencia,* this main line was a five-inch rope stowed on her after deck which was intended to support a breeches buoy which could be used to haul passengers and crew to safety.) As far as it was possible to determine, she was equipped as the law and regulations required.

Of her three decks, the saloon deck was mostly open to weather. Below was the main deck, and below that the lower deck. On the upper, or saloon deck, were two series of cabins. The so-called "hurricane deck" was located on top of the aft series of cabins. The "fiddler's deck" was located forward on top of the forward cabins. (Although referred to as "decks," the last two were merely the roof of upper deck cabins.) The lifeboats were carried three on each side, the two forward ones hung in their davits along the fiddler's deck, the two aft ones were in line with the hurricane deck where the liferafts were also stowed.

The pilothouse was on the saloon deck at the front of the forward series of cabins. Just aft of the pilothouse on a level with the roof of the cabins was the bridge, and just aft of the bridge, which was about 100 feet from the bow, and on the same level was the charthouse. Her average speed was about 11 knots.

Her passenger list reflected the society of the day. It ranged from merchants to the newly elected supervisor of Seattle's schools, from mothers with their children to an alleged criminal, Pat Hogan, who was thought to be involved in a hold-up in Vancouver and who had fled to San Francisco.

He decided to return home to vindicate himself of the charges and became one of the passengers.

As with Pat Hogan, fate played her merciless game on others, causing some to miss the ill-fated steamer, others to embark at the last minute on a voyage which was to become their final journey. The *Seattle Times* reported several accounts of passengers' fortune and misfortune.

One was Mrs. William Smith of Vancouver, B.C. After first expecting her husband to be on the steamer, she had received a telegram from him that he had barely missed the boat in San Francisco. Another was R. A. May, a fireman on the *Valencia,* who had a quarrel with the steward just before the boat sailed on her previous trip to San Francisco and left, his life probably saved by this minor dispute. Scores of others would not be so fortunate.

After passing out of San Francisco Bay, the *Valencia* turned north up the coast, giving a wide berth to the capes and reefs of northern California. Under normal circumstances she would have continued north a few miles offshore, and turned east after passing Cape Flattery into the Strait of Juan de Fuca towards Victoria and Seattle.

The *Valencia's* voyage north was quite ordinary. The fine weather continued and she should have reached Cape Flattery at the entrance to the Strait of Juan de Fuca sometime within a few hours before or after midnight on Monday, her third day at sea. The passengers kept busy playing cards, reading, or lounging on deck, wrapped in blankets against the cool winter temperatures. According to testimony given by surviving Second Officer Peter Petterson, the trip from San Francisco to Cape Mendocino was made on the usual course and mostly within sight of land.

At Cape Mendocino, which the *Valencia* passed about half past five Sunday morning, the California coast turns from a northwest to a more northeasterly direction. It was common practice to now lay a course to Umatilla Lightship, 14 miles south of the entrance to the Strait of Juan de Fuca. The *Valencia* followed a course of approximately "north 20 degrees west," or 340 degrees magnetic, and maintained this course until 9 p.m. the following night, which was Monday. The course actually indicated on her bridge by the compass was 342 degrees, and reflected a westerly deviation of 2 degrees. Unknowingly, the

The *Valencia* and, inset, Captain M. Johnson. After she ran ashore, waves demolished her superstructure, leaving survivors clinging desperately to the ratlines that ran up her masts.

The photo of Captain Johnson, above, and some others to follow are of poor quality because they had to be copied from microfilm. The originals and the *Seattle Times* in which they appeared have all been destroyed.

steamer was on a course straight for the Graveyard of the Pacific, the treacherous region of surf-beaten rocks which continued to reap a rich harvest of unfortunate mariners.

A little over a month before the *Valencia* sailed, two vessels had been wrecked close to where she was heading. On December 13, 1905, the British ship *King David* was blown ashore near Bajo Reef off Nootka Island and wrecked. All hands reached shore safely, but later seven men were sent by lifeboat to find assistance. They were never seen again. Maybe they had been picked up by the *Pass of Melfort* which ran ashore not far away with the loss of 26 lives, but no one knows.

According to mariners, 1905 had been a record year for disasters in the area. Many other vessels were damaged or wrecked during the fall and winter season. Among them were the steamers *Portland* and the *Nell*. In addition, many sailing schooners and smaller sailing vessels were reported lost and never heard from again. The *Valencia* was about to join the tragic list.

On Sunday in late afternoon, Captain Johnson stood bent over the chart table in the pilothouse. He was of medium-build, with blue eyes and a rather large mustache which dominated his face. He had a strong nose, and his receding hairline was carefully covered by hair combed forward and parted in the middle. He picked up his pen and noted in the ship's logbook that Cape Blanco had been passed at 5:20 p.m. that afternoon. The Second Officer, however, later was of the opinion that this entry was largely conjectural. He would testify that no one on board, including the Captain, had actually seen Cape Blanco.

Sunday afternoon about three o'clock, before the vessel passed the illusive and invisible Cape Blanco, the wind blew lightly from the north. Now it clocked around and became a strong breeze from the southeast in front of an approaching low pressure system. For the remainder of the voyage the southeasterly wind continued. Although no fix or "point of departure" had been obtained north of Cape Mendocino which was seen early Sunday morning, and no lights or land observed since, the Captain did not begin soundings until 6 p.m. on Monday. From then until 9:30 p.m. soundings were taken every half hour, but no bottom was found. According to Second Officer Petterson, the logbook, which was subsequently lost from the wreck, had simply indicated that at each sounding 240 fathoms of lead line had been cast out. Assuming the vessel was proceeding at about 11 knots and allowing for the slant of the sounding wire, the readings indicated that she was in at least 80 to 100 fathoms. There was no reason for alarm.

Around 9 p.m. on Monday, Captain Johnson evidently felt that he was near the Umatilla Lightship. It had been dark for hours with most passengers below in their cabins. Many were probably preparing to leave the vessel and began packing their belongings since officers had promised them breakfast in Victoria the following morning.

It was the usual custom on this route for navigators to pick up the lightship as reassurance of their position, either by sight or by soundings, which was possible by a peculiarity of the sea floor. The known position could then be used as point of departure from where to lay a course for Cape Flattery. But Captain Johnson did not really know his position. From the testimony of the Second Officer, the only survivor who could give an accurate account of what happened on the bridge, it became clear that Captain Johnson used as his "point of departure" a theoretical position where he thought the vessel ought to be, having no knowledge of where she actually was. This decision was a grave error.

At 9 o'clock that Monday night the log showed that the vessel had run 652 nautical miles. Had this distance not been greatly influenced by winds and current, it would have indicated a position roughly opposite the Umatilla Lightship. But for a reason which will remain forever unexplained, Captain Johnson stated to Second Officer Petterson that the log was "over-running." By this statement he meant that the vessel had not travelled as far as was indicated by the log.

He stated to Petterson that "the log over-runs by 6 per cent." What he meant was that if the log at 9 p.m. on Monday showed a distance of 652 miles, the vessel had actually sailed only 612 miles over the ground. This theory would have placed the vessel about 40 miles south of the Lightship. Both Second Officer Petterson and the Fourth Mate had doubts about the Captain's assumption, and suggested to him that he might be mistaken. But the Captain assured them that they were wrong and he was right.

As already noted, the log, because of its design, measures only the distance travelled through the water by the vessel towing it. If, because of ocean current, the water moves with the ship, the distance travelled over the ground or past some fixed point will be farther than the distance indicated by the log. By contrast, the reverse is also true. If the current is flowing backwards in relation to the vessel's motion, the distance travelled will be less than indicated by the ship's log. Because this knowledge is very basic, it seems unbelievable that Captain Johnson could have been mistaken in his interpretation of the log. Unfortunately, he was. The only plausible explanation for this error was the fact that Captain Johnson had made the trip up the coast once before, when he took the *Valencia* north to Alaska, but at a different time of year. This previous trip was during the summer, when the Davidson Current can be absent, or even run to the south, and the Captain could have assumed the current to be similar during winter. That this was not so, however, was clearly indicated on pilot charts of the North Pacific Ocean.

These pilot charts are predictions of weather patterns and ocean currents likely to be encountered for each month of the year. The one for the North Pacific Ocean, January 1906, shows currents running northward close along the coast from Cape Blanco over the entire course of the *Valencia* from one to three knots. But as was later discovered, there were no such charts aboard the *Valencia*.

The Captain now turned the steamer eastward toward the coast. His assumption that the log had over-run was terribly wrong. It must be assumed instead that the log under-ran. While it showed 652 miles run at 9 o'clock Monday night, the strong northerly current which prevails in winter had given additional speed to the vessel – and the log. Instead of being 40 miles south of the Lightship, as the Captain thought, she was probably at least opposite it – or even to the north.

Because Captain Johnson believed that he was much further south than he was, about 9 p.m. he turned eastward towards the coast. He also took constant soundings which was customary in order to pick up the entrance to Juan de Fuca Strait. Although the sounding to 9 p.m. had shown no bottom, he obtained a sounding of 80 fathoms about 9:30 p.m. At 10 o'clock he sounded again. The depth was now 60 fathoms.

He changed course again, turning slightly toward the west. According to the Second Officer, this was the usual course taken from Umatilla Lightship to Cape Flattery at the entrance to the Strait. Captain Johnson obviously still believed that he was somewhere near the Lightship at about 10 o'clock that Monday night.

At 10:30 p.m. a sounding indicated there was still 60 fathoms. At 10:45 p.m. the sounding was 80 fathoms; at 11, again 60 fathoms. From then on, the bottom quickly shallowed. At 11:15 the sounding was 40 fathoms; at 11:30, it was 30. This decrease in depth not only should have made the Captain very uneasy, but also should have been a strong warning that something was dangerously wrong. These soundings were not at all characteristic of the run from Umatilla to Cape Flattery.

It seemed as if Captain Johnson now indeed felt that there was some problem. At 11:35 he changed course sharply to starboard, away from the coast of Vancouver Island. This change could indicate that Captain Johnson had a vague feeling of being on the B.C. side of the Strait. One passenger later reported that around midnight somebody had seen a lighthouse, which could have been the light at Carmanah Point on Vancouver Island. This fact was never investigated, and Second Officer Petterson never mentioned a lighthouse during his testimony. It is possible, however, that Johnson had seen it and thought it to be the light on Tatoosh Island. Consequently, he might have turned right to enter the Strait. But now a 11:45 sounding gave only 24 fathoms. Something was terribly wrong.

Within 10-15 minutes Second Officer Petterson, who was on the bridge with the Captain, saw a dark object ahead. The lookout posted at the bow of the ship must have been asleep. Being a full 100 feet in front of the bridge, he should have seen the rocks and cliffs first and signal this to the bridge, but no such signal came. Petterson immediately alerted the Captain, who ordered the wheel hard over, throwing the bow towards the east, but to no avail. Within minutes the *Valencia* crunched to a grinding stop. Captain Johnson exclaimed in horror:

"My God! Where are we?"

CHAPTER TWO

Lifeboats Become Death Boats

The *Valencia* first struck a rock, or ledge, a few hundred yards off shore. She hung there a few minutes. She then turned on the rock as a pivot, and came off, drifting slowly ashore in the mountainous swell. She now lay at almost right angles to the shore, her bow pointing out to sea, and her stern only a few yards from the cliffs. This was to be her final resting place.

Her passengers and crew were marooned near the rocky shore, waves crashing against the steep cliffs. Wireless radio communication was in its infancy, not available to either the ship or people on land. On this uninhabited and remote coast, there was no one to hear their cries for help. There now began a 40-hour drama, horrifying in scope.

Captain Johnson could not have picked a worst place to be wrecked. Cliffs 100 feet high dropped almost vertically into the boiling sea, each wave exploding with a roar onto the rocks, throwing spray high into the trees.

The testimony of the survivors all agreed that the stern of the steamer came to rest only about 15-30 yards from shore. According to reports which have been published over the years by divers who have been on the wreck, the distance seems to have been from 15 to 20 yards, not 30 – a maximum of 60 feet.

Within a few minutes of the vessel grounding, soundings were taken in the bilges of the middle compartment. Water was rising in the holds at the alarming rate of one foot a minute. The Captain evidently came to the conclusion that the vessel was going to sink, and therefore should be beached. He informed Second Officer Petterson of this decision. The engines were put full speed astern, ramming her into the rocks stern first. It would be over 15 hours before the outside world learned of the disaster, the *Valencia* and those on board left alone at the mercy of the sea.

Soon after she struck the lights failed as the generators were drowned in the rising water. The darkness heightened the

Of the survivors who escaped the vessel, many died on the wave-battered rocks near Pachena Point, above and below. The ladder in the photo below was built from driftwood by three of seven fishermen who survived when their boat was wrecked in 1940, but who were trapped at the base of the 60-foot cliffs. The photos were taken by the late Jack Hunting. He and his wife, Jean, lightkeepers at Pachena Point for 35 years, built an excellent reputation for helping shipwrecked mariners.

panic that passengers and crew felt during these first confused moments. Spray was blowing over the vessel with each onslaught of another big wave, ramming into the disabled vessel with relentless fury.

Captain Johnson's next order was to lower the boats to the saloon rail and lash them there. He explicitly did not want them launched at this time. What followed would be called later "a disastrous failure in the use of the boats." And this was indeed an understatement.

The transcript of the hearing held before two Seattle Inspectors on January 27, 1906, contains over 1,000 pages of testimony from the few survivors. Although the testimony often differs in some detail or other, it produced the most important account of the tragedy.

At this inquiry, Second Officer Petterson gave a vivid account of what took place in the first moments after the *Valencia* ran aground. He testified that after Captain Johnson said "hard to starboard" he had "run to the telegraph and put hard to starboard, and the same time the mate gave 24 fathoms of water."

Q. After you saw this black object?

A. Yes, sir. The mate was just coming after we put hard a starboard and reported 24 fathoms. The ship swung around a bit; in a few minutes, a very short time, she struck. When she struck we put her full speed astern, at the time the Captain sung out, "You run and get soundings, go get the carpenter."

Q. The last order for soundings was after she struck?

A. When he gave it 24 fathoms, he told the carpenter to go and take soundings.

Q. After the sounding of 24 fathoms, did you sound again?

A. No, sir, no more. I think there was somebody sounding afterwards but I am not sure. I believe the Fourth Officer was sounding when I came on deck but I am not sure. The First Officer reported one foot of water.

Q. This sounding, after she struck and the Captain ordered soundings, this was soundings in the holds, you mean the sounding of the hold?

A. Yes, sir. One foot of water. Then the carpenter came running, two foot he said, then in a few minutes he reported six feet of water. Then the Captain called all hands on deck.

Q. Was the ship backing at the time?

A. Backing still when the carpenter came up. The last I heard was six feet of water. He said to me: "Sing out all hands on deck," all the people were nearly on deck when I left the bridge; come around with life preservers on them, of course, when we first struck they all jumped out of bed.

Q. Did you back the ship afloat after she struck first? You say your ship struck immediately after you had 24 fathoms and you put her full speed astern, did she back off the rocks?

A. Yes, sir. She went off in deep water, you could see her going astern.

Q. You were backing when she struck the second time?

A. I could not say that, I was not on the bridge, I was working with my boat aft.

Q. Were the engines reversed with ahead motion?

A. Not that I know, sir.

Q. Did she strike any more?

A. No, she didn't strike, not that I can recollect.

Q. Don't you remember when she struck and hung?

A. She hung right in deep water ... the Captain said to me: "I am going to beach her," that is the last words he spoke to me. Then when I run aft, there was a lot of cabbage on the hurricane deck aft when I run up, on the steps, I fell right backward on my back on the main deck alongside the main mast. [Apparently cabbage had been part of the cargo, and the crates had broken open.]

Q. What threw you down?

A. I just slipped on the steps. Then when I come to the boat, two men were there with the boat ready to clear the falls, in a few seconds two more came, then we got the boat over the rail, about five of us; we swung the boat out and we lowered the boat down to the rail and made the boat fast.

Q. What boat was that?

A. No. 5 boat, after boat on the port side, [Petterson must have been mistaken here, as the No. 5 lifeboat was located on the starboard side, and later mentioned by boatswain McCarthy as the boat he got away on. The boat was probably No. 6.]

Q. That was your station. Had you been aboard ship long enough to have a boat drill?

A. No, sir, and hadn't been since I been on her....

A sketch which appeared in the *Seattle Times* shows the disastrous consequences of launching the lifeboats at night. Between 40 and 60 passengers and crew drowned in the first 30 minutes. The only surviving officer was Second Mate Peter Petterson, top right.
Below: A Lyle gun similar to the one carried on the *Valencia*.

Petterson then went forward on the starboard side, where "a lot of women were." He asked for five or six of them to get into the boat he was looking after. Although these lifeboats were designed to hold 18 people, later tests were to show that the boats could carry 22, but they actually felt crowded even with 18 on board. As Petterson's testimony continued, the investigators learned how most of the lifeboats were lost and, as was later concluded, mostly due to the lack of proper commands from the Captain. In the darkness and confusion of the first half-hour after the wreck, no one was sure who was an officer or a passenger. As Petterson's testimony revealed, the following 30 minutes would result in the loss of many lives:

A: I got five women in the boat, two of them said "No, we don't want to get in the boat, we might as well stay by the ship." At this time I was standing in the boat myself for the wind came up, it rolled pretty heavy, the boat started to swing but I put my fingers in the wire netting in the rail for to keep the boat steady; I was singing out to people that was in the boat to give me a hand to keep the boat steady, but nobody tried to do anything to it. There must have been eight or nine men in the boat, I could not say whether they were sailors or not; it was dark, could not see anything. There came a cry: "Lower all the boats!"

Q. Where did that come from?

A. I could not say. I said: "Don't lower the boat, keep it by the rail, don't lower the boat!" But, anyhow, in a few seconds the boat went right underneath my feet, they lowered the boat underneath my feet.

Q. How many were there in the boat at this time?

A. There must have been seven or eight men and three women. Two of the women got out. I was hanging alongside; I was going to let go, I had sea boots on me, and one man came along, he tried to get me over the rail, but he could not do it alone. He sang out for another fellow, he came and gave me a hand and I got back on the ship.

Q. You hung with your fingers in the netting when the boat was lowered under you?

A. Yes, sir.

Q. Was the ship afloat now?

A. I think probably; she didn't roll any more, just a little bit.

Q. You don't know who lowered the boat?

A. No, sir, I do not. They sung out from the hurricane deck "Come back with the boat" but I don't know who that was. I sung out myself: "Come back!" She was headed right out against the sea, must have been headed right about south; the sea started to break over both sides and the boat was headed right out to sea. Then, after that I run up on the bridge and the Captain was standing there on the starboard side; then I did not see any more boats, all them boats, some of them, must have been capsized; I didn't see any more boats.

Q. You don't know what took place with the boats forward?

A. No, I do not know anything what happened to the other boats.

Q. These people that were in the boat, did they get in with their own free will, or were they ordered in the boat?

A. I took five women in the boat, the others got in themselves, because my idea was not to lower the boat because I knew when I left the bridge that the ship would not sink in deep water, so I knew there would be no danger.

Q. You don't know whether this order to lower emanated from the bridge or whether it was some panic?

A. I don't know who gave the order to lower the boats.

Q. Your boat went into the water alright, and unhooked everything alright; all the equipment and everything was intact?

A. The plug and everything was in the boat before we put it out at all. I says to the sailor: "See if the plug is in the boat," he says "It is in the hole."

Q. Was this a wooden boat?

A. Metal boat, had two plugs.

Q. What kind of plugs were they?

A. Screw plugs.

Later on there were some questions raised about these plugs. Some of the survivors claimed that the plugs in some of the boats had been missing, and some boats apparently had the wrong plugs in them. They would not fit the hole. It seems to be likely, however, that as the passengers were not familiar with the way the plugs were to be put in and secured, in the panic and excitement they just were not able to install them in the proper fashion. Still, one boat did not have a plug, and a "little naval boy, Willets," who was among those who made it to shore, kept holding his hand over the hole in the bottom to prevent the inrush of water.

Petterson's testimony continued:

Q. When you got to the bridge the boat forward had been lowered and smashed?

A. Something like that; I didn't see any boat when I came forward.

As was learned from Petterson's testimony, no boat drill had been held on board the *Valencia*. Out of the total crew of 65, only 32 had been on her previous voyage. Although a fire drill had been held on that passage, only two of the lifeboats were swung out and lowered. Consequently, only two boat crews were familiar with the boats and their tackle. Additional confusion arose because many of the seaman had no idea to which boat they had been assigned. In addition, the lights had gone out, and the wind and driving rain added to the chaos. As a result, the witnesses were not sure exactly where they were at the time, and what happened next.

Certain facts, however, emerged from later testimony. It seems clear that Captain Johnson's orders were not carried out as he intended. He had ordered the boats lowered only to the saloon rail and lashed there until further orders. But he did not check on the execution of his order. For some unexplained reason, one-half of the seamen – the men best fitted to handle the boats – stayed below decks awaiting further orders, while several of the boats had already been lowered and capsized.

Boatswain Tim J. McCarthy was one of the survivors, and his testimony painted a dreadful picture of these first terrible minutes. First he was asked about conditions on board immediately after the grounding. He told the Inspectors that he had been down below when the *Valencia* struck. He also testified that the weather that afternoon had been very thick and hazy. The seas were running high out of the southeast, and had done so pretty much since Sunday morning. The Inspectors then wanted to know about the loading of the first lifeboats, and he was asked if these boats were loaded with passengers and crew while they were hanging on the davits – the pair of curved metal arms at the side of the ship from which the lifeboats were suspended. McCarthy replied:

COLONIST EXTRA

VICTORIA, B. C., JANUARY 23, 1906

S.S. VALENCIA WRECKED NEAR CAPE BEALE

BETWEEN 50 AND 60 LIVES LOST --PATHETIC SCENES ABOARD

125 PERSONS STILL ON VESSEL WITH DEATH STARING THEM IN THE FACE

Headlines in the special edition of *The Colonist* newspaper at Victoria and three of the survivors. Boatswain McCarthy, one of the sailors who desperately tried to summon aid, is at left. The others are T. Lamson and J. Marks who was on the bridge when Captain Johnson severely burned his hands lighting distress rockets and later blew off two of his fingers.

"Yes, sir. The moment the covers and strong backs were taken off, they were piling in from all directions. The Captain had already given orders not to lower the boats below the saloon deck rail; then I got the crew together – one quartermaster, one watchman and one deck boy. It was so dark you could scarcely tell a sailor from a passenger, only by his voice."

He then explained what happened to No.1 Lifeboat:

"No. 1 boat, the forward one on the starboard side, instead of easing the backstay away they let it go by the run, and all the davits broke off short, right at the nibs of the skid. It must have been a passenger that slashed it away with his knife, because if the davits were four times as strong they would never have held them with that sudden jerk."

When the passengers rushed into the boats, three of the others were cockbilled in the same fashion; that is, one end was dropped suddenly before the other, and all the occupants were spilled into the sea. Only one of these passengers survived.

In two other cases, the boats were successfully lowered and launched. But each one had only one or two crew in them. They were soon turned broadside to the waves and capsized. Out of 20 or 30 people in these boats, about a dozen managed to get ashore. Of them, nine survived, forming what later was called the Bunker party. A third boat seemed to have been launched about the same time, but she probably capsized as well. No one survived. In addition, one of the three liferafts somehow slid overboard and was lost.

A terrible human drama unfolded aboard the doomed steamer during these first few minutes of utter confusion when the boats were swamped and crashed against the side of the steamer like eggshells. A little boy was seen standing crying by the rail on the saloon deck, vainly asking for his mother, who had been swept to death from one of the lifeboats. Two men who escaped drowning when the boats were first swamped managed to reach the high bluff, some 60 feet from where the steamer was held by the rocks. They were unable to climb the cliffs and, shouting for help, were pounded to death on the shore.

A lady, whose husband had got into one of the boats, tried to hand her child to him, but the ship lurched violently just at that moment and the infant fell into the sea and quickly disappeared. The father was also drowned when the lifeboat overturned. One of the passengers, a miner from Alaska, walked around the ship offering $1,800 in gold to anyone who would take him ashore. No one would listen to him. He finally threw his money on the deck. The gold was in a bag which rolled and slid around the deck of the dying steamer. Nobody bothered to pick it up.

A Mrs. Stoltenberg from Bellingham was on board with her two children. Mother and daughter perished, but the boy survived, for a while at least. Another passenger, an old man, was lying down on his coat when a child nestled close to his side and asked to be taken to his baby cousins in Seattle. His last name was Stoltenberg, and he told the old man that his mother and sister had drowned. He would not survive either.

The terrible consequence of the mishandling of the lifeboats was that less than a dozen people made it to shore. Probably between 40 and 60 of the passengers and crew were drowned within the first 30 minutes in various accidents to the boats. Only one lifeboat was now left on the steamer.

The loss of most of her lifeboats because of the lack of proper orders and confusion during the first critical minutes was the first in a series of tragic mishaps. Next morning, for instance, the last remaining boat reached shore with little difficulty. It then became clear that if the boats had not been launched at all until Tuesday morning, they most likely could have saved a substantial number – if not most – of those on board. The terrible failure in the use of the boat equipment was due, in part, to lack of proper drill and, in part, to the order from the Captain to lower the boats to the rail. This position made it possible for the passengers to get into them without proper crews to see that they were correctly launched and manned.

But some people had survived the launching of the lifeboats. One of them was a passenger, Charles Samuels, who testified later at the hearing:

Q. What position did you hold aboard the *Valencia*?

A. First class passenger.

Q. Where were you when the ship struck?

A. I was in my cabin with three friends. We had all four took one cabin, and we were talking there telling stories, because they first tell me about 12 o'clock they tell that we can see a lighthouse. I been the first man on deck when the vessel struck. When the first wreck was it most turned me overboard, I was like catch my arms around the boat and hold myself, then I went in the parlour.

There were mostly ladies and children in the parlour; they didn't go to bed, it was 12 o'clock already.

Q. Where were you after the boat struck?

A. I was on deck, first man on deck.

Q. What did you observe then?

A. I went into the parlour to the ladies.

Q. Did you hear any orders given from the bridge?

A. None at all.

Q. Did you hear any orders to lower the boats?

A. I heard the Captain holler "Lower the boats," then I went into the parlour to the ladies and helped put on their life preservers, on children and ladies.

He continued to testify that there had been lots of life preservers, every passenger had one on his bed. When he was asked if he heard any of the ladies asking to get into the boats, he answered: "No, they were very quiet."

Q. What did you get away from the ship on?

A. The first launched boat, No. 2.

Q. Were there any ladies in that boat?

A. Mr. Campbell's wife and daughter, 14 or 15 men, and when they launched the boat down the little lifeboat smashed on the steamer and the people got scared....

Q. Did they crowd to get in the boats?

A. I saw people run for the boat and I jumped in and after Mr. Campbell and his wife landed in the boat, the boat was launched down to the water, we had no officers at all. The oars were all tied together and we had only pins [bottom pins to fit into the oar locks] to stick in it and the pin broke off, the wood pins were left in the hole and we could not make any other go in. Sitting in that boat load, we could not do no work at all, we didn't understand very much, we had no officers, five or six men in the water. Came out on the other side the trees, the cliff; a minute later, came big wave, went slap in the face and throw the boat, didn't hit in the water and landed out to the cliff; I hold on helpless; I could not help nothing at all, it was dark, afraid to get back down to the water.

Couple minutes later came a couple of fellows together. Mr. Bunker and Mr. Campbell, Frank Richley and myself, we were all four laying on the cliff and close together. We lost everything, hats and shoes, and the rain was running down from the cliffs down our necks.

Q. How did you get everybody up to the top of the cliff?

A. We waited to light of day. Afterward I went with Mr. Bunker to find a way to go up on the cliff....

Q. Did you get to the cliff right opposite where the ship was?

A. Yes, sir.

Q. How long did you stay there?

A. From ten to twelve minutes, not very long. We started off to go right away.

Q. If there had been a line shot ashore, could you have got it up there?

A. We could not got it any place. The people from the steamer didn't know we were there, we could not get any signals at all.

Q. How far were you from the ship this time?

A. About 250 yards.

Q. Could not they see 250 yards? Could you not wave something, to let them know you were there?

A. We could not do anything and the matches were wet.

Q. Could you see the people on the ship?

A. Yes, sir.

Q. Didn't the people on the ship see you?

A. I don't believe they saw us.

Q. You people all left as soon as daylight came did you?

A. We saw in the middle of the night all kinds lights, green and red lights from the steamer.

Q. What did you leave for?

A. To look for a trail, some place to go in, because we were all wet.

They finally struggled to the top of the bluff slightly north of where the stern of the ship was facing the cliffs. They decided to walk westward and turned left. This decision doomed the 100 or more survivors still on the *Valencia*. Had they turned right they might have been able to reach the cliff directly behind the steamer, which was less than 1,500 feet away. As was later proven, the *Valencia's* Lyle gun could have fired a line and those on shore easily pulled across the five-inch line from the steamer. It is almost certain that with the breeches buoy everyone could have been pulled to safety.

CHAPTER THREE

Wholesale Murder

In the meantime, throughout the night on board the ship there was little panic after the first shock of the impact. Although many of the passengers rushed to get into the boats, their action was understandable because the boats had been lowered apparently for that purpose, and there were no officers to restrain them and to tell them otherwise.

During the night, Captain Johnson set off several rockets to attract attention, and also to get a better view of the coastline. A sailor named John Marks was on the bridge with the Captain. He later testified that the Captain's hands were burnt and bleeding, but that he still sent up signal after signal until the powder was so wet that it would no longer ignite. Another witness testified that two of the Captain's fingers had been blown off by a rocket.

Marks also reported that bed clothing and linen of every description was soaked in kerosene and burnt during the night. Women had given even their underskirts to the sailors to burn from the top of the aftermast to try and attract the attention of passing steamers. But it was in vain. No one came to their rescue.

On Tuesday morning it was evident that the *Valencia* was breaking up. Although her hull seemed to remain comparatively intact, the forward cabins and pilothouse, the charthouse, and the bridge were beginning to disintegrate from the seas washing over her bows.

About 8:25 a.m. Captain Johnson asked for volunteers to take the last lifeboat and try to make a landing. He was hoping that the men could take a line which he was going to fire from the Lyle gun. Incredibly, there was no response. No one, passenger or crew, stepped forward. What happened during these moments on board is told by some eyewitnesses:

According to Boatswain Tim McCarthy "... we took the heaviest snatch block we could find, with a good five-inch strap and hooked it on to the mainmast head and snatched this five-inch line.

"Took the Lyle gun out of the rocket box abaft the bridge, and the whole apparatus, and had it right aft handy, before we left at all, this was ready.

"So the Captain says, he says, 'Tim,' he says, 'Will you go in the boat?'

"I says 'Yes, sir,' because before that the forward part of the bridge, it was see-sawing up and down ... and part of the midship house – there was iron around the fiddler – the four beams were banging around; that is the four beams were adrift, and anything loose went whacking up against the house, and swinging over the ship's side.

"So at this time it was low water, at least we thought it was and I am pretty sure it was, too, and as the tide started to come the sea was making on the tide; you could see one sea making higher than the other, making all the time. But there didn't seem to be any more wind. So he says: 'If we can get a boat out through the breakers and make the land somewhere abreast of the ship you make your end fast ashore and I will use all the passengers and help here, with the two watch tackles, and set it up, and see what we can do that way.

"So I said 'All right' I said. 'If I can get a crew I will go.' "

The Captain looked around. There was no reaction. Not a single hand went up. The men were staring at their feet, hands in their pockets. After a few seconds the Captain cleared his throat. "Well," he said, "By God, Tim" he said, "If you go, I will go with you myself." That seemed to break the ice, and brought the men back to reality. All of a sudden, help was offered. "Yes, I will go too," said Mate Holmes.

McCarthy continued: "I says 'All right.' So the sailors at first didn't care a whole lot about going, but finally one consented, and they all said 'Yes, yes, yes!' I could have got a boat load then. So the Captain just picked out so many and he said: 'Do you want to take them?'

"I said 'Yes, I think they can handle an oar.... If they can't they are no good in the boat.' So we had six oars, a rudder, two boat hooks, three pins on each oarlock, a bailer, and we had everything that belonged to her outside of the rockets. The rockets we used in the dark that night trying to attract attention; we had burned them. So we got into the boat. The Captain,

Cape Beale Lighthouse, the rocky shore and cliffs typical of the region. The vertical tree gives an idea of the height of the cliff.

Chief Engineer and the First Officer stood on the saloon deck and were ready to have the boat lowered down as soon as I said the word. They said: 'You say the word whenever you think you can see a chance.'

"I said: 'All right!'

"We got into the boat and got our offshore oarlocks shipped, and so I shipped my oarlock for a sculling oar – for a steering oar; so I watched those seas roll in and I saw two or three good ones come in, and I thought there would be a chance to get out between those; we might catch one of them; I thought I could get over to them, but I was sure to hit one before I could get over, and sure enough I did.

"One sea combed and almost pitchpoled us – stood us right on end – if she hadn't been a good boat, she certainly would have. Just then one fellow broke his oar, the fellow pulling the bow oar. So I kept sculling and steering at the same time, and I worked her out, and when I saw I was outside of the surf, then I hollered to the gang, and in fact we all hollered and they let out a good hearty cheer, and we thought everything was all right, and I said to the fellows, 'Now, sit on your oars and go to it for all you are worth and we will go down the line.'

"So we pulled along toward Cape Beale; in fact at that time we did not know where we were, but we pulled in that direction anyway, followed the beach. We thought we could see a place now and then where we could land, but My God, there was no such a thing as a landing. So I guess we pulled along the beach for over three miles, it must have been. We had the wind in our quarter and the sea was almost abeam, a pretty good strong tide. All of a sudden I could see some rocks loom up away off shore, so I says to the fellows: 'Here we are! We are about two miles from Neah Bay!'

"I took those rocks for Duncan, off Tatoosh Island. There was a little island there that looked the same as Waddy Island inside of Tatoosh Island itself, off Cape Flattery. So I kept between this rock and we got just about half way and it started breaking and then I noticed it was something unusual because I have been through there as often as I have hairs on my head, halibut fishing, off Cape Flattery, and I never saw it break except in very bad weather.

"It is a good passage between the rocks and the island for any ship, except in bad weather. I thought it was something unusual because I never saw that before. Just then a good sea hit us a wallop, and slewed around broadside on and three of them lost their oars. That left us with two oars. So finally, we got over that and we saw a little cove making in, and we thought we would get in there, and we could not make a landing exactly where we expected to, and so we started in to pull back towards this little island, again ... and we finally saw that the beach was quite smooth and sandy – a good sandy beach, no rocks. So then I said to the fellows: 'It is a good sandy beach and we can try it here, to see if we can make a landing. If we get a couple of bumps we can stand it!'

"So they said: 'Alright, if you think it is all right we will try it.' "

The men in the boat had rowed for about five hours, and were exhausted. "Pretty well gone," said McCarthy. They were soaking wet, and without proper clothes. Some of them had a cork jacket on but were told by McCarthy to take them off so "...that they could roll out of the boat better." McCarthy finally said to them: "Now we will watch a chance and we will go in on this sea, and if we should happen to hit the beach, be ready to jump before the boat turns over and kills us!

"So they said: 'All right.'

"So we kept these two oars going and the other fellow steering – I had this fellow Marks steering and I was steering with a little drag [sea anchor] in my hand – holding a drag ready to throw it overboard to hold her end on to the sea. So, as luck happened, I didn't see any that I thought I would need this drag for. So the sea hit her a good wallop; and fired us away up in the woods, and by God, we got ashore and never got our feet wet. And that was the last of the boat racket. That was about five minutes after one...."

Q. And you landed then?

A. Yes.

Meanwhile, on board the foundering ship, the departure of that last lifeboat Tuesday morning had installed renewed hope to the survivors. The Lyle gun was made ready, and in anticipation of the prompt arrival of the crew on shore, Captain Johnson ordered the gun fired. To the great disappointment of passengers and crew, the first attempt was unsuccessful. As the line paid out, it chafed through against the side of its box. The projectile carried with it only a few feet of line, leaving the rest onboard.

Carmanah Point Lighthouse where Daykin and his party left to give assistance
but did nothing when they arrived at the wreck site.
Below: The headlines in the *Seattle Times,* **January 27, 1906.**

But the second shot was successful, the projectile carrying the line far over the cliffs and into the woods and, as was later discovered, even clearing the telegraph wires, embedding itself in the soft forest floor. This was a thin line, perhaps about a quarter-inch thick. Now those on shore could pull across the heavy five-inch-thick rope which had been fastened to the mainmast. Passengers and crew waited with anxious hearts for someone to appear at the top of the cliff, so close, to take the line in and provide an escape.

But hour after inactive hour passed. Suddenly, their hopes were crushed. A groan of despair arose from those watching in horror as the thin rope, chafing against sharp rock, parted. There were no more projectiles left. The frayed end of the broken rope disappeared into the sea, severing another opportunity to survive their terrible fate.

While this drama was unfolding on the *Valencia,* Tim McCarthy and his men were desperately trying to get help.

They tried to follow the beach back towards the ship, but could not find any trail. The underbrush was so heavy, that McCarthy didn't think it possible "... to make it in a hundred years." The party decided, under McCarthy's order, to walk along the beach as far as they could, hoping to somewhere find help. They took the sail from the lifeboat, which might later be used as a tent, an ax, and a few biscuits. Because the beach was covered in logs and other driftwood, and the men cold and exhausted, progress was slow. Finally, they came to the mouth of the Pachena River. They tried to wade across it, with McCarthy leading. Soon he was up to his knees. Then he suddenly sank into quicksand and barely got out.

The group then started towards the woods, and back again to the beach, looking for some opportunity to get inland. Finally, they found a cabin almost at the edge of the trees. It was weather beaten and water soaked and obviously had not been lived in for years. As they looked the cabin over, noticing plenty of animal tracks in the vicinity, one of the men suddenly exclaimed: "By God, I think there is a trail in here!"

The men scrambled forward. The trail was overgrown and hardly noticeable, but it was clear that it had seen some traffic in the past. Within five minutes the group now came upon telegraph wires and a few minutes later spotted a white signpost with black letters: "3 miles to Cape Beale."

This sign was the first indication the men had that they were on the Vancouver Island shore, the last place they had expected to be. They started along the trail to the west, following the wires. After a while they came upon another trail, this one running in a north-south direction. The men were puzzled. Then they noticed more telegraph wires, a double set branching off to the north and south, as well as another trail. They decided to follow this new trail south, and soon stumbled upon cow manure on the path. Within minutes they saw Cape Beale Lighthouse.

The lighthouse keepers – Mr. and Mrs. Paterson, accompanied by their big dog – ran out with their children. To the surprise of the shipwrecked men they said: "You are the shipwrecked crew!" McCarthy wondered how they could know, Then Mrs. Paterson said: "I was so sorry we could not connect with you!"

The men were baffled. What was she talking about?

"Were you not trying to talk to us from further along the line?" Minnie asked, now wondering herself.

McCarthy answered: "No, we have never done no talking. We are off the Pacific Coast Company's boat the *Valencia* that was wrecked along here. I don't know exactly how many miles it is; she is laying in this direction anyhow." He pointed to the east.

"There is over 100 lives aboard it at the present time. I want you to get in touch with Victoria or Seattle for to get assistance! In fact, wire everywhere!"

Mrs. Paterson was still confused and asked again. "Did you try to tap that wire along the line somewhere?"

McCarthy replied: "No, ma'am."

"Well, about half an hour ago somebody was trying to get us on the line, but all we could understand was 'telegraph'."

Suddenly it dawned on them that somebody else must have got ashore during the night. Later they would learn that it was the Bunker group – nine men who had survived the capsizing of the lifeboats.

Back in the house, Mrs. Paterson immediately tried to reconnect with anyone still out there. Once contact was again established, she instructed the men to tighten some loose telegraph wires. Finally the connection improved greatly and every one heard the words: "My name is Bunker."

When Mrs. Paterson did not at first understand the name, and asked to have it repeated, the voice on the other end crackled through the wire: "Do you remember the famous Bunker Hill? That's me and I've lost my wife and children."

Bunker told Mrs. Paterson that they were nine in the party. There were six more passengers and two firemen with him, and they were in pretty bad shape. Bunker didn't think they could last much longer. Mrs. Paterson immediately contacted Carmanah Lighthouse and then told Bunker that men were on their way towards them carrying dry clothes and provisions. Mrs. Paterson noted that the lineman, Joe Logan, who was with the party from Carmanah, was a very good man who "will die on the trail before he gives up."

During this time on board the *Valencia,* the almost 100 survivors barely clung to life, with little hope of rescue. There was one hero among those left on the ship. His name was Joe Cigalos, a Greek fireman. In his broken English he gave touching testimony to the investigators:

"So when it got daylight, the Captain, he shoot a gun on the land to get line ashore, but nobody to take it; if somebody was there to take the line ashore, it be all right, everybody saved alive."

Q. Did you see no one ashore on the cliff?

A. One fellow on the beach, on the rocks, there, and he tried to get up but can't get up, too high; it was straight up rocks underneath.

Q. Could this man get up on top of the cliffs?

A. No, he could not swim, he no could swim to get some place to get up.

Q. What became of him?

A. He died there some place, he could not get out.

Q. Did you see no one else up on the side of the cliff?

A. When he shoot the line had no more leads to shoot. Every gun go about 5 miles with the rope [he obviously did not know about the distance that can be bridged with a Lyle gun, which is closer to 1,000 feet], but they got nobody to help us. I don't know, the same day the boatswain, he take a boat with six sailors, I don't know Captain give the order. I don't know, he got away alright to help us so, same time I see the boatswain take boat away, I say, "My God! He'll go down!" I don't know what we are going to do, and then them lines was gone alto-

Greek fireman Joe Cigalos received a medal for his bravery which included trying to swim to shore.
Below: The Paterson family at Cape Beale. Mrs. Paterson stayed at her post for three days and nights answering calls from anxious relatives. The following December she became a heroine when she played a major role in saving the crew of the sailing ship *Caloma*. Her rescue effort involved walking along five miles of rough trail, wading through chest-deep water and crawling through thick wet underbrush. She received a medal and a silver plate for her heroism but never fully recovered from the ordeal and died five years later.

gether. There was no more leads or nothing. I was standing looking, the people were on the deck, I was real sorry, I say, "My God! God help us!" Nobody can do nothing!

I take my coat off and my vest, I say "God help," I'll try, if I can do my best.

So I told him [the Third Engineer] to make a line fast behind, so he made it fast, I don't want the line big, I take a thin line, tell him to give all the slack he can get, no break the line. Had line enough to go five, ten miles, enough to go to top anyway. Well, when we got the line fast, I forgot my knife, in my pocket, I get my little knife, small one, and open it, then I was wait because the sea get a little smooth, to get a chance to jump, the big sea never came all the time, every few minutes. I cross my hands on myself, I say "Good bye!" If I am alive to get a line ashore every body will be happy; so the Third Engineer, I told him what he going to do when I go in the water, so he told me, "All right, John!"

I tell him when I go in the water you see me sink the line and pull the line, you pull me, he say "All right!"

I cross myself, I say "Good bye, boys." I jump overboard and swim hard through the surf, by that I jump overboard, had to look sea no cover me up, sea was full of sticks, boxes, and everything; so then I try to swim, slack the line and so a big sea wash me back, I dove under so I was very close but I can't catch my hands because too much suction, it was me out again.

Then these sticks, everything turn the line and I took my knife out; a big stick, heavy stick, hit me on the head so I get headache that time, I looses my senses enough, so I take my knife and get it off right away.

I got clear, but when I got clear I got my hands make it fast under my arm and round my wrist and fingers ... so I try to get to shore again, but the sea was so rough, if I cut the line to go out myself I might go but I was sorry for the other people, if I lose, I lose myself, if I am alive every body all alive, I do not want to be alive myself, and I am sorry, so any way I can't land myself. I let the line come altogether from my hand because when they pull [the line] aboard, so many sticks they may kill me.

I left the line, I was swim hard because when I left the line to get to boat so I could swim, the tide, the current run so, you know, take me south on port side ship, so I swim hard to get —

I try to go behind on the stern so they throw life buoy there, so I get close, couple yards, ten yards, I say, "Please throw that life buoy to me;" he had it in his hands and he throw it to me, because before I go overboard I told him to get it ready for me, so he got pull me aboard again, so when I got aboard the people don't know what going to do. They give me little whisky to warm me, take my clothes off and some man give me socks, and put coat and overcoat on me and lie down in top bunk.

Before I started to swim their room was gone and people were on top of the poop and some were behind because big sea come and break the rooms; very few rooms left, might be four, don't know how many was. So any way Chief was with me in the room and the Freight Clerk altogether. An old man gave me five dollars. So the engineer and clerk they waiting every minute for the ship to break up, so I tell him should not be sorry, might be some steamer come help us. Captain, Boatswain, Chief Mate were look in some mattresses and dry things to burn to make light, some ladies take skirts; dry things to put fire to signal to some ship to help us.

The First Methodist Church in Seattle later collected over $100 from the congregation for a medal for the Greek fireman's bravery. Reverend Fletcher Wharton had told about his remarkable act of heroism during his Sunday service, and the congregation had been deeply affected. The Reverend said:

"Is the man not worthy of a reward who, when he was drawn on board the steamship exhausted and in awful suffering, refused as a fitting climax to his former deeds, the offered stimulant, saying: 'Give it to the others'?"

On one side of the medal was Cigalo's name, a record of what he had done, and the name of the donor, while the other side simply said: "He did his best." Unfortunately, this tribute did not apply to many others involved in the rescue.

Subsequently that day, another attempt was made by an officer to swim ashore with a line, but he met with the same fate, and finally had to be pulled back aboard.

By Tuesday afternoon news of the wrecked steamer had finally reached Victoria and Seattle. That day, January 23, the *Victoria Daily Colonist* distributed an extra edition headlined:

"S.S. *VALENCIA* WRECKED NEAR CAPE BEALE
BETWEEN 50 AND 60 LIVES LOST
PATHETIC SCENES ABOARD

125 PEOPLE STILL ON VESSEL WITH DEATH
STARING THEM INTO THE FACE"

Also Tuesday afternoon around 3:30 p.m., a telegraph message was received at the Seattle offices of the Pacific Coast Steamship Company by Mr. J. E. Pharo, the assistant to the manager. The message from Victoria read simply that a vessel had gone ashore somewhere on the west coast of Vancouver Island. About five minutes later a second message stated that the vessel was the *Valencia,* and that she was ashore somewhere west of Carmanah Light. Captain James B. Patterson, the company's Seattle port captain, was also in the office at the time and assisted Mr. Pharo in his preparations for rescue.

Knowing that the *Queen City,* one of the large passenger steamers belonging to the same company, was due to arrive at Victoria shortly, orders were sent at once to Captain Cousins to land his passengers at Victoria and to proceed immediately to the wreck. Mr. Pharo also attempted to find one or more seagoing tugs, knowing that a light-draft, easily handled vessel would be of most use in the rescue work. Unfortunately, the only suitable vessel in Seattle and the immediate area was currently under repair and out of service.

The Puget Sound Towboat Company, however, informed Mr. Pharo that they undoubtedly had tugs near Neah Bay and within 25 miles of Cape Flattery, which put them also within about 25 miles of the wreck. Tugs were stationed in Neah Bay almost continuously, waiting to tow incoming vessels up the Straits. At that time the government telegraph line from Neah Bay to Port Angeles was out of order, however, and no contact could be established. This failure had dire consequences for those still alive on the *Valencia.*

The situation was extremely frustrating for those who wanted to help, as a seagoing tug could have reached the wrecked steamer within a little over two hours, still in daylight on Tuesday afternoon. They at least could have established some communication with the people on the *Valencia,* and would have had more time to plan a rescue.

By Wednesday morning, when those on the *Valencia* were still alive but despairing of rescue, papers throughout the continent and as far away as New York City had reported the tragedy. Headlines across the country screamed at their readers:

"APPALLING DISASTER!"

"LOST!"

"THOUGHT ALL ARE LOST!"

The *Seattle Times* in Wednesday's edition charged:

"GOVERNMENT'S AWFUL NEGLECT"

and later, on January 27, shocked the public with the headline,

"WHOLESALE MURDER." As events unfolded, this headline would prove to be a mostly accurate assessment, although for quite different reasons.

The papers now were quick to criticize the U.S. Government. They charged that it was the apathy and lack of interest the United States Government had for years displayed toward the signal station telegraph it maintained from Tatoosh Island Observatory to the Mainland which was to blame.

The *Times* went on to say that every season staunch vessels were driven to their doom by raging storms in this vicinity, and precious lives had been lost in similar instances because the government line was down. Articles like these were responsible for the incredible public outrage over the next few days as the drama continued.

The *City of Topeka*, another vessel belonging to the Pacific Coast Steamship Company, was at the critical time in Seattle discharging dynamite. When news of the wreck came, Mr. Pharo ordered the unloading speeded up. Soon learning that it would be impossible to finish unloading before late that night, he ordered the captain to immediately proceed to the wreck. The *City of Topeka* left about 10 o'clock Tuesday night, having on board Mr. Pharo, Captain Patterson, nurses, a doctor, various medical stores and 17 extra seamen. Also on board was staff reporter and photographer Davidson of the *Seattle Times*, who would later return with the only photographs.

In addition, as soon as the first bulletins of the disaster were received, the Canadian wrecking steamer *Salvor* was prepared for sea. She was lying at Esquimalt near Victoria, and left at once in the company of the salvage tug *Czar*. The *Czar* eventually arrived near the wreck, but in a display of cowardice and disregard for human life which will remain a lasting blotch in Canadian Maritime history, abandoned the helpless people on board.

Back in Victoria, about 5 p.m. on Tuesday, Captain Cousins, in command of the *Queen City*, had landed most of his passengers and headed for the scene. The vessel arrived off Carmanah Light about 10 o'clock that night. From the information at his disposal, Captain Cousins thought that the crippled liner was located about four miles west of Carmanah.

Again, fate conspired against the unfortunate people on the *Valencia*. That Captain Cousins did not continue towards the scene of the accident that night was another tragedy because both vessels likely would have been able to at least make visual contact. If nothing else, he could have stood by within sight of the people still on the wrecked vessel, reassuring them that they were not totally forgotten, that help would arrive with first light.

But during the remainder of that night the *Queen City* drifted or cruised around near the mouth of the Strait of Juan de Fuca. Only at 7 a.m. on Wednesday did she proceed westward along the shore, making contact by signal with Carmanah Light on the way. She was then informed that the wreck was still 18 miles further west. The *Queen City* also passed the *Salvor* and the *Czar*, both vessels having obviously spent the night in a manner similar to the *Queen City*.

Keeping within a mile or so from the coast, Captain Cousins sighted the *Valencia* about 9 o'clock Wednesday morning. He now hove to, about a mile and one-half from shore.

CHAPTER FOUR

Nearer My God To Thee

There was an eerie silence on board the dying ship. Here and there the huddled forms of the desperately cold and frightened people were visible in the first grey light of early morning. The wind was ice cold, and light rain was falling, Most were seeking warmth from each other, together in small groups, covered by wet blankets. They had spent a terrifying night. Everyone knew that the crippled liner was quickly disintegrating under the sea's onslaught. In the darkness they had been forced to the top of the hurricane deck, taking shelter as best as they could. A few men had stayed in the comparative comfort of the remaining cabins underneath that deck in the afterhouse.

Outside, women and children were lashed to the rigging, out of reach of the sea. It was a pitiful sight, some wearing only their night dresses and with bare feet, trying to shield children in their arms from the icy wind and rain. Others had climbed into the freezing ratlines as well, lashing themselves in place with clothing, blankets, pieces of rope or whatever they could find, hoping to escape the frigid waters. But most still remained on top of the hurricane deck, under blankets and shelters of tarpaulins. They sat there, cold and afraid. The cries of the gulls mixed with the groaning sounds of the ship as it was battered to pieces. Bang – bang – bang – a steel cable which once held the funnel in place hit the remnants of the bridge, almost gone now. The seas had calmed a little, but as the ship settled lower and lower through the night, the waves still hit her bow with a hollow crash, climbed over the bulwarks, and rushed up the inclined deck.

It was frighteningly obvious that the final hour was near. Less than 30 yards from shore, passengers and crew were as helpless as if they had been in mid-ocean. Safety was really so close, but they knew that an attempt to reach it meant certain death against the jagged rocks or drowning in the surf that relentlessly crashed into the cliffs just behind.

The reef-studded waters of Barkley
Sound and the liferaft at Turrett
Island containing three bodies.

Hour after hour they lived an agony of dread and futile hope. Only those who believed in miracles could have thought now that aid would still reach them in time. Huddled in the upper works of the vessel, the waves breaking beneath them, the human forms whom death had hesitated to claim were now waiting for the end. Among them were husbands who had seen their wives drown almost in reach of their hands, and mothers who had watched their children swept overboard into the dark cold sea. There were officers, including the Captain, who were still reassuring their passengers, but fully aware of their pending fate.

Soon, all of the remaining passengers and crew were forced to the hurricane deck or into the rigging. With every wave, water was pouring into the afterhouse on the saloon deck, while much of the upper works had already been swept away. Then came what seemed a miracle. About 9:30 a.m., just as another futile attempt was about to be made to swim ashore with a line, a vessel appeared on the horizon. The Captain quickly had the Lyle gun on the aft deck fired three times in case she failed to see the *Valencia*.

The sequence of events as they unfolded now was so totally unbelievable and heartbreaking that only the words of one of the few remaining survivors can reveal the feeling of crushed hope, disappointment and despair experienced by those on the broken liner:

The Greek fireman said about these moments: "...when the *Queen City* come everybody was happy; they holler that everybody be all right when they land alongside. The *Queen City* stop over there about a mile or two; the next I see another boat come in, the *Czar* tug boat; after the tug boat come the *City of Topeka* behind, one boat behind the other that way! So the sea was awful rough and the *Czar* went to the *Queen City* and reported to tell the Captain what are you going to do. He was alongside talk with the Captain, talk about the *Czar*, he turn around and come right up to the *Valencia*; everybody thought he was coming for us, but when he was little closer, half mile or so, sea was so awful rough break right from forward to aft, sea was in all the rooms any way."

Q. Over the *Valencia* or over the *Czar?*

A. Break over the *Valencia*. So it was in all the rooms any way, and that smoke stack and that iron casing in the smoke

The *City of Topeka* and the *Queen City,* below, were both seen by the cold and desperate survivors on the *Valencia,* but neither vessel attempted to save them.

The *Czar* and the *Salvor*. The *Czar* had the best chance of rescuing the 80 or so survivors but sailed away and left them to die.

stack down below, they were all going behind that because when the big sea were strike —

Q. The iron casing around the smoke stack?

A. Yes, sir. When that is gone the sea get a chance and go right over. It was about 50 in top of the mast head, they were signalling; something hit the mast head and broke the top mast off, so when that one gone I see people fall down, five or six, every body grab ropes, nobody got killed, but some body tell me second mate, he say to me, he got killed, fell down in the water, second mate he was between the two irons. After that the *Czar* see the mast fall down everything washing, turn around back again to go away, scared of the rough water of losing himself.

Q. It was rough then was it?

A. Yes, sir, it was ten to one that a loaded boat can't get out, if you put ten boats through there you would lose nine, you would get one alive may be; I don't think you can go any boats through there any way; so it was awful rough, because *Czar* he big boat can't get there, I don't think a row boat can't get there, because it was awful rough sea. I see the *Czar* go away, he started outside to look up *Queen City* and talk with the Captain.

[During this conversation, the captain of the *Czar* apparently told Captain Cousins on board the *Queen City* that he had seen no survivors on the *Valencia*. Having been as close as he was, it is impossible that the frantically waving people on the hurricane deck and in the rigging could have escaped his attention.]

The fireman continued: "...I don't know I say, 'My God!', it take too long, I guess nobody can help her, because she was awful rough weather, so I was thinking myself, I tell myself, I say, 'My God!' I was in the water yesterday I can't get ashore if I stay till the last minute; too many, too many people, so bad, grab me by neck lose myself, too, I say best to take the liferaft, so before they throw the one liferaft overboard, about half past nine, don't know how many people, I was try to get myself, because the third assistant, he say, 'Come on, John,' I had no chance to go because the liferaft was too full you know so I stay aboard and the liferaft nearly go inside, the poop broke between." [He is referring to the "poop," or aft deck, which caved in. According to other testimony, about 10 or 15 people fell into the hole at that time, but most managed to climb out again. Some of them went aft, and some crawled into the rigging.]

"The Captain he say: 'Boys,' he say, 'there is the last chance, go on the raft, get something to go on the raft.'

Captain Johnson pleaded with the women, but they refused and said that they might as well die on the ship as on the raft. One of the passengers begged his wife to get into the raft, but she refused as well. At this time the ships which apparently had come to their rescue were still clearly visible, and the women must have assumed that they soon would be taken off without having to risk their lives in the frail-looking raft.

The raft remained fastened alongside the vessel for perhaps 10 or 15 minutes. Unanimous evidence of the survivors was that the Captain, officers and some of the passengers kept urging the women to go on board the raft, telling them that it was their last chance. But to no avail.

Finally 17 more men got into the raft, including Joe Cigalos and Second Officer Petterson, and the Captain said: "You might just as well go this time," and turned away. The women were singing the hymn "Nearer my God to Thee," the Captain looking seaward towards the vessels that were ignoring his disastrous plight. He was heard saying: "My God! Send relief to my passengers!"

The steward Walter Raymond was probably the last survivor to leave the doomed ship. He recalled that the last raft was just being launched when he hurried past one of the stewardesses. He stopped to urge her to go, but to no avail. He paused for a moment before taking his plunge into the sea. He remembered that they looked at each other for a moment, and she asked: "Are you going, Walter?"

He nodded his head. The stewardess, smiling bravely at him, opened her lips and with a voice choked with tears joined the other women in singing. The steward, steadying himself on the few strands of remaining rigging, jumped into the sea towards the tossing raft which had already left the side of the ship.

About 80 people were still left on the wrecked steamer, staring at death with terrible certainty.

But even those on the raft were far from safe. They began a desperate struggle – not to be swept onto the barnacle covered jagged rocks and certain death on the surf-lashed shore.

After an hour of desperate rowing, they succeeded in escaping the all-consuming surf into calmer waters offshore. When they looked around, no more ships were in sight.

Cigalos kept telling the men in his raft not to head out towards the ocean because they would all freeze.

"I told them to go back again; to go to find a good place on the beach to land ashore; so some people, he say, 'No, try to go to the ocean,' I say, 'My God! You got to die?'

"I try to do the best I could, 'I don't want to die, you don't want to die!' I take a little rest because I was so tired, and I see the *Topeka*. I said, 'Hurry up, boys,' somebody say, 'Come on, boys,' everybody pull like Indians, because it gets dark, it get foggy...."

The *Queen City* had blown her whistle four times in a salute and left. Incredibly, she had not tried to assist the dying steamer and its human cargo. The *Czar* had also left. The *City of Topeka* remained just beyond the horizon, although the desperate people in the boat could not see her.

About the same time the port raft left, the one on the starboard side had also been launched. This raft had been half hanging over the gaping hole in the deck, making it difficult to get ready. But with the Captain's help, it was finally launched and got away. Only a few men were on board when the raft was launched, everybody else apparently feeling that they would be rescued by the *Queen City*, much safer than trusting the risky raft. But as the raft left, a few more jumped from the rigging into the frigid waters and climbed on board in a last desperate struggle to escape with their lives.

This raft broke through the surf with little difficulty. The men on it soon caught sight of the *City of Topeka*, but were unable to attract her attention. They drifted west in the current and landed around midnight Wednesday on Turret Island, about 17 miles west of the wreck. This island is part of the Broken Group at the entrance to Barkley Sound. Like many others, Turret Island was small and thickly wooded, a few Indians the only inhabitants.

The conditions on this raft, as later told by the survivors, reflects the terrible state of mind of the shipwrecked people on the *Valencia*. Physical and mental exhaustion of those in the raft would claim victim after victim.

The first was Engineer Wilson. He jumped overboard almost within reach of the Island and was drowned. The remaining nine occupants landed on the Island. Before morning, five had gone crazy and jumped into the water as well. All drowned.

Another survivor, a waiter named Frank Connors, imagined having seen a lighthouse and wandered off into the bush. Indians alerted the *Salvor* which had accompanied the *Czar* but had not approached the wreck, about the survivors on the Island. Captain Ernest F. Jordan was an officer on the *Salvor* at the time and later recalled: "I took a boat and went in search of the missing man [Frank Connors] and in search of the raft.

"The raft I located; but there was no response to our calls along the shoreline of the little bay where the raft had beached. We made a second tour along the beach, as close to land as possible. Then, just by accident, we spied Connors hanging on to the branch of a tree. He was in bad shape and was raving mad when I reached him, and I had almost to tear him from his clutch of the tree – I suppose the poor fellow imagined he was still clinging to the rigging. We did what we could for the survivors and on arriving at Victoria sent Connors and another guy, Long, to hospital, where they recovered. The particular raft – or the people on it – had been piloted by Sam Hancock, the head cook of the *Valencia*. He did a good job."

The cook, who had already survived four shipwrecks, had been lucky for the fifth time, despite his premonition of doom on the day the *Valencia* left San Francisco.

Survivors later spoke very highly of the bravery and conduct of the stewards and stewardesses on board the *Valencia*. They had constantly passed meat and sandwiches to the people on deck and in the rigging, urging them to hang on just a while longer.

At Cape Beale, meanwhile, Boatswain McCarthy and the men who had arrived there the previous afternoon spent the night with the lighthouse keepers. All through the night the Patersons had sat up, watching the telephone in case there were new developments. The new day dawned rainy, with a strong breeze still blowing. The people at the lighthouse looked at the sky in resignation, knowing that the weather would only make the plight of those on the *Valencia* more hopeless. The seas were running high.

McCarthy said: "Mrs. Paterson, I guess it's all off, there is nothing left now ... this Bunker party and us are pretty lucky, I guess are about the only ones to tell the tale."

"Yes, I am afraid so," Mrs. Paterson agreed. She was shaking with exhaustion and in great despair.

At the investigation later in Seattle, McCarthy testified that on Wednesday morning the *Salvor* and tow boat *Czar* had steamed in to Bamfield Creek.

Q.. Had you gone back to the beach then?

A. No, sir, I was at the lighthouse all the while; Mrs. Paterson says, "We will have news now pretty soon now, here comes the *Salvor* and the tow boat."

Mr. Paterson was not too sure and thought it wasn't the *Czar,* but it was. We were anxious to start out all the while; she said: 'No use, you can't help them a particle!' she says, 'We have done everything that can be done, there are two parties started out now; just as soon as they get up Bamfield Creek we will wire down and find out what they know.'

That was done, and they were told that the ships had passed the wreck but could not get close enough to her to tell whether there were any passengers left on her or not.

McCarthy continued: "I mentioned this house aft on [the] saloon deck, and house on hurricane deck, asked them if they thought they were still standing. They said the two masts were standing and as far as they could understand, the houses were also. I says, 'If the houses stand it, the people stand it, they can live on it two or three days as long as the houses don't get away.'

"Then we said to Mrs. Paterson, 'Could you get us a pilot from Bamfield Creek, we'll start out!'

I says, "By God! I mean to start out and I'll take my crew with me, even if you cannot get us a pilot to show us the way along the trail, you have not got anything to give away I guess, we can get plenty at Bamfield Creek." Those people get their stores once every two months or so, they told us they were running short, she kind of persuaded and told us, "You can't do a particle of good by going along there, I have done everything possible...."

The *City of Topeka* had arrived alongside the *Queen City* about 11 a.m. on Wednesday under the command of Captain Cann. Captain Cousins informed him that there was life on-

The *City of Topeka's* lifeboat towing the raft of survivors, so crowded it is almost sinking.

board the *Valencia,* that they had seen three puffs of smoke. Astonishingly, Mr. Pharo from the Pacific Coast Steamship Company now ordered the *Queen City* back to Victoria to continue on her regular voyage. Equally astonishingly, the *Salvor* and the *Czar* had already departed for Bamfield, making no attempt to help the disintegrating steamer and its huddled survivors. Now only the *City of Topeka* was left.

But in an incredible display of poor seamanship by two captains, the *Queen City* had neither given, nor had the *City of Topeka* asked for, compass bearings to the *Valencia.* Because of the blustery weather and poor visibility, the wreck was not in sight when the *Queen City* sailed away. As a consequence, the *City of Topeka* never found the *Valencia* during the rest of that day or while there were any survivors on board.

After the *Queen City* left, the *City of Topeka* slowly steamed toward the coast until about one mile off, where she obtained soundings of some 11 fathoms or 66 feet. The captain now thought it unwise to go any closer and proceeded to patrol the coast in search of the wreck. She apparently travelled as far to the west as Cape Beale, and even as far east as the wreck, but no one saw it.

Around noon, however, she sighted the first of the two rafts that had left the *Valencia* that morning. She was now about four miles west of the wreck.

The desperately cold and exhausted survivors aboard the raft included Joe, the Greek fireman. He has already described the terror of those last hours of the disaster and their horror and disbelief when the *Queen City* blew her whistle and departed.

"I take little rest because I was so tired," he later testified, "and I see the *City of Topeka....* I was scared if it get dark, because if it got dark there he can't see the liferaft. We had no light and we had no sign, everybody was pulling. I was trying to get head to wind all the time to sea, wind was to starboard; somebody hollered: 'See the boat, see the boat,' it goes up and down; a sailor on the *City of Topeka* he say to the Captain, liferaft there,' some body says, 'That no liferaft,' he say, 'that fish, whale or something....' Everybody hollering, the sailor he hear us, he go to the Captain, he say, 'Mr. Captain, people on liferaft.' The Captain he put glass and look, he say, 'That's all right.' The Captain turn around toward us; everybody was hol-

The almost submerged raft alongside the *City of Topeka*.

lering and the Captain, he hear too, he blowed three whistles, when the ship turned around he blowed three whistles, every body was happy because they saw us. I was like myself to get warm. When it come alongside I say, come a little farther, come close, every body so tired...."

The condition of the survivors was desperate. They were half frozen and almost unconscious from exposure and exhaustion. The raft was barely afloat. As the men in their water-logged raft battled to reach the *City of Topeka*, a lifeboat was lowered from the vessel. It was in charge of the second mate, Burke, who finally managed to secure a line to the raft. But the survivors were still not safe.

The sea ran heavy. One minute the two small vessels were high in the air on top of a giant wave, the next they disappeared from sight in the trough.

Finally, the boats arrived alongside. The staff photographer of the *Seattle Times* froze this moment forever in one of the few photographs of the disaster. The drawn expressions on the men's faces tell the tale.

In the stern of the raft sat an old man with snow-white hair and pallid features, holding onto his place. His name was Charles Allison. Three others were lying in a heap in the rear, washed by every swell, held in place only by the bodies of their companions. Time and again big seas swept over them, sending a shudder to the bystanders on deck who feared they would still be swept away by the sea. Then came the problem of getting the survivors out of the raft and up the steep boarding ladder onto the ship.

The men on the raft were too exhausted to assist in their own rescue, so near death that they could not even tie a rope to themselves. Once, when the raft gave a lurch, it looked as if the old man with grey hair had been washed away. Fortunately, they finally got him up on deck. But just as the old man was being rescued, another man was swept away. He, too, was rescued from the freezing waters by quick action from the rescue party. Another man had an even more miraculous rescue. He was swept from the foundering raft but managed to grasp a line and cling to it. He was then hoisted up the side of the ship. About half way his strength gave out and he plunged back into the sea. He was also saved by the crew of the ship's lifeboat.

The lifeboat crew from the *City of Topeka*. Their bravery saved several of the survivors from drowning.

The survivors, even though closer to death than life, were the lucky ones. One of them was the steward Walter Raymond. When he left, some 80 scared human beings were still on the wrecked steamer. There now was no hope of getting off the *Valencia* alive.

CHAPTER FIVE

The Terrible Betrayal

The last witnesses to the final moments of suffering by those remaining on the *Valencia* was the shore party which had left Carmanah Light immediately after hearing the news by telegraph on Tuesday afternoon. Included were assistant lighthouse-keeper Phil Daykin from Carmanah Light, lineman Joe Logan, and a trapper, Joe Martin. While Daykin graphically reconstructed the immense tragedy of these final moments, the conduct of this group raised many questions.

They had left the lighthouse at Carmanah Point on Tuesday afternoon, taking with them "some line and provisions." They had been advised that two men apparently were still trapped at the bottom of the cliff, unable to scale the high walls. The rope was intended for their rescue. No other equipment to possibly help the people on the *Valencia* was taken.

They reached the Clanewah [Klanawa] River in the evening. They spent the night on the river and, according to their testimony, did not leave again until about 9:30 in the morning. Unbelievably, around noon they had a cup of tea at an Indian ranch, even though only a few miles away men and women were in the final hours of their lives, tortured by despair after watching three ships sail away without any attempt to aid them.

Soon after leaving the Indian ranch, the party arrived on top of the bluff overlooking the wreck. At the inquiry Daykin testified:

Q. How long after you got to the bluff overlooking the wreck was it until she broke up?

A. I couldn't tell, exactly; it was between then and one o' clock.

Q. Did you consult a watch at all?

A. No.

Q. You don't think it was over an hour after you arrived until she broke up?

Frank Bunker and, below, white-haired survivor C. Allison. "Why did you run away?" he asked Bunker at the hearing. "All we wanted was a single man on top of the cliff to catch a line!"

A. No.

Q. Could you hold communication with the people on the wreck?

A. Yes, I think so, if we had wanted to. If there had been any reason to do so I guess we could; we could have hollered.

Q. Did you holler at all when you got there?

A. They gave a cheer when we got there, and we answered.

Q. Did they ask you anything about anything you may have had along with you?

A. No, they didn't ask anything. There was no word spoken you could understand at all.

Q. You could hear the voices?

A. Quite plain.

Q. Could you hear them plain enough to have distinguished what they were saying, any articulation?

A. I think if any one man hollered anything out we might have heard it.

Q. You didn't distinguish any particular words, or anything of that kind?

A. No.

Q. You simply heard the cheer come up?

A. Yes.

Q. Did you have anything in your party, any ropes or anything you could throw to the wreck?

A. Yes, no, we had about a hundred feet of line with us; we took it along to where we supposed the two men were on the bluff.

Q. Did you make any attempt to throw the ship's small line back to the ship?

[They had found the end of the line which had been fired ashore with the Lyle gun the previous morning. As already noted, this line had broken, one part slipping back into the water, the other end remaining on the bluff. This line could have been used to extend the one they had brought along. But for whatever reason, this solution did not occur to any of the three men.]

A. I tried to make an attempt, but saw it was useless; the line tangled; you know how the rocket line is coiled; she tangled right up.

Q. Did you try to throw your line to the wreck?

A. No, it was not long enough.

Q. How far from shore did the stern of the wreck lie?

A. I should judge between 200 and 300 feet, I haven't been to the wreck since that; I have not been to the wreck since the time I was there

[Daykin's ability to judge distances was later seriously questioned, as he largely overestimated the distance to the stern of the ship. At the time of the inquiry several weeks had passed, and it is possible that he had second thoughts about what he should have done. Making the distance seem larger might have been intended to remove some of the responsibility for not rendering help when it was so desperately needed.

[Many statements and testimony agreed, further ascertained many years later by the location of the wreck by divers, that the stern of the steamer was only about 15 or 20 yards from the rock face. Because Daykin and his group were on top of the bluff and about 100 feet above the sea, with a rock tied to the end of the rope, they should have tried to throw a line to the people on the steamer. But they didn't.]

Q. Couldn't you arrange the line so it wouldn't tangle?

A. I don't think so.

Q. You didn't make any attempt to do that?

A. No; I didn't think I could have thrown it far enough, either.

Q. Did you see the crash when it finally came? That is, the sea that finally broke up the deck and broke the deck houses up?

A. Yes.

A last big sea ran over the boat. The masts collapsed and the *Valencia* spilled her remaining human cargo into the freezing water when she folded like a jackknife. The three men on the bluff saw many people drifting seaward, clinging to wreckage. They could still see them about half a mile westward of the breakers, having come safely through. Twenty or more survivors were desperately hanging on to whatever they could grab. All were wearing life preservers, and when the ship disintegrated they had clambered for some piece of wreckage as the tide took them out to sea. But the rescue ships had all left. Even the men on top of the bluff walked away; not even waiting until they lost sight of the last clinging human form; leav-

Some of the survivors, the arrow identifying Frank Bunker.
Below: The *Lorne's* lifeboat crew searching for bodies.

ing to their fate the people who were so desperately waiting for help from their fellow human beings on top of the bluff.

Within a few days of the sinking, newspapers printed more and more details as information became available from survivors of the tragedy. Searching for and identifying the dead was the first gruesome task. For several days mutilated victims were picked out of the water and off the beaches and rocks in the vicinity. Serious questions already were being raised about the circumstances leading to the accident.

Captain Johnson came under attack, as did the Pacific Coast Steamship Company and the disastrous rescue efforts. Questions were raised about Johnson's competence as a mariner, the lifesaving equipment on the ship, and the failure of any of the ships standing by to render assistance. They all were guilty of breaking the unwritten law of the sea – providing every possible assistance to those in distress – thus condemning to death some 100 men, women and children.

There was the first shore party led by Frank Bunker, as well as the trio consisting of Daykin, Logan, and Martin from Carmanah Lighthouse. Both groups failed miserably in rendering effective assistance when they could have saved many lives.

Captain Johnson's conduct as master was seriously questioned. As Captain he failed utterly and with terrible consequences. He atoned for his initial negligence after the *Valencia* hit the rocks but by then it was too late. He then offered assistance whenever he could, and never once thought of leaving as his vessel was battered to pieces. He went down with the ship a true Captain, paying the ultimate price for his tragic mistake in navigation.

On January 27, 1906, the *Seattle Times* printed a short article, "Capt. Johnson came from Shop to Sound." Questions were raised about Johnson's competence as master. The public was stunned to learn that, until four years before, he had been a resident of McKeeport in Pennsylvania. He had apparently lived there for 17 years, working in the tube mills. He had then moved to Seattle and then to Port Townsend. The article went on to note, however, that Johnson had experience as a seaman before going to Pennsylvania, but that his sea-faring experience was gained as a boy in the Swedish Navy. In addition, his final wreck was not his first. It had happened four times before.

Oscar Marcus Johnson was 40 years old at the time of the tragedy. He was born in Norway and came from a seafaring family. At 14 he shipped before the mast in the Swedish Navy. Although one report credited him with being with the Pacific Coast Steamship Company for 15 years, it is unclear how that was possible since he had lived in McKeeport. This article went on to say that Johnson was "highly regarded" as a mariner by the company and previously had only one accident. It had occurred the previous season on a voyage while going to St. Michaels in Alaska and also with the *Valencia*. This had been his first trip on the coast. His record was contradicted by other reports, however, which claimed that his last wreck had been his fourth, and not his second.

He was described by one of his brothers to be a reliable and conscientious man, who neither drank nor smoked, and who was deeply devoted to his profession.

On January 25, a day after all on the *Valencia* had perished, Johnson's wife was still hoping for his return. At their Seattle home she was reported sitting with their little daughter looking out of the window towards Meigg's Wharf. She said to a reporter: "I always used to wave to him from this window. He has been through so many storms before, I am sure he will come home all right. My husband is a strong swimmer, and I am sure he could make shore."

But he didn't. Johnson's body was one of the many which was never found.

The Federal Commission of Inquiry into the *Valencia* disaster had no doubt in their assessment of Captain Johnson.

According to their findings, whatever may have been the explanation for Captain Johnson's mistake in navigation, it was the fundamental cause of the disaster. When the vessel struck she was at least 30 miles farther northward than Captain Johnson supposed she was. This discrepancy was found to be almost entirely due to his failure to allow for the current and the following wind. Their final verdict was that Captain Johnson failed to take the proper action of heading immediately out to sea until he could confirm his position. Upon his improper navigation had to rest the responsibility for the disaster.

Within hours after the *Valencia* ran aground, another similar incident almost took place. The steamer *Edith*, also driven off her course by the strong northerly current combined with the southeasterly winds, almost ran ashore within a short distance of where the *Valencia* struck. The difference in one vessel being wrecked and the other saved was the *Edith's* captain. When he found that he was not certain of his position, he turned sharply out to sea and cruised around until he was able to confirm his position.

As already mentioned, among the nine passengers who escaped was Frank Bunker. He was a professor, on his way to Seattle with his family to take over the position of Superintendent of Seattle Schools. The newspapermen at the *Seattle Times* quickly realized that here was a man with an exceptional education and reputation, and whose opinions were therefore readily accepted by readers. He immediately became the focal point and spokesman for the survivors, his opinions at first widely accepted.

During the inquiry, however, it became obvious that though he was a highly recognized figure in public life, his judgement in matters pertaining to the accident was extremely questionable. It was the action – or lack of action – of his shore party which later came under heavy attack for abandoning the people on the *Valencia* in their hour of need.

All nine survivors in his party had left the *Valencia* in the two first launched lifeboats. One included Bunker, Richley, and a few others. The other boat left at the same time with 15 passengers, eight of whom drowned during the first few minutes when it capsized. Although Bunker later asked in one of his published outbursts why the landing party under Boatswain McCarthy had only six people in this lifeboat, his own boat had left the *Valencia* with no more. According to Bunker himself "very few, no more than six or seven." Of them, only Bunker and fireman D. F. Richley survived.

It was Bunker who charged "Wholesale Murder" which made the headlines of the *Seattle Times* on January 27. In Bunker, the newspapermen had found a true treasure, a respected citizen who had lost his wife and two children in the tragic accident. His was a voice that Americans wanted to believe in. The photo of him holding his daughter appeared on the front page next to the accusing headline.

The conditions under which Bunker had lost his family were very tragic, and gained him the sympathy of all. With his wife and two children he had climbed into the second lifeboat

Young sailor J. Willits testifying before the Seattle Commission and, below, some of the *Valencia's* crew. Six of them died.

to leave the *Valencia*. There were no officers or seamen in the boat and it immediately capsized, throwing everyone into the sea. The boat then righted itself, although almost filled with water. Bunker managed to get back aboard, finding his wife clinging to the side. He pulled her in and looked for his children. The girl was gone, but he found his boy. As the *Seattle Times* on January 27, 1906, reported: "... my little girl was gone, but the boy was there, though limp. At this point the occupants were Richley, myself, my wife and the baby in her arms.

"The seas washed over us every moment but I put my finger in the little boy's throat and rolled him on my knees. He began to cry and called: 'Papa!' My wife said she could not hold on longer. I kissed her goodbye for I thought it was all over with us all.

"I chanced to look up and for the first time saw a dark shadow a few hundred feet away, which I felt sure was land. I then realized we were in the surf. I told my wife to hold on a moment longer and we might yet get through. I held her with one arm and the baby with the other. In a moment came a terrible crunching impact with the rocks.

"I still held to my precious ones.

"A second wave knocked the boat against another rock then something struck me on the head and I lost my hold. At the same moment the boat turned over and we were again in the water.

"I was dimly conscious of being thrown up two or three times and then thrown back on the rocks, the last time with just strength enough left to cling to them and make my way a few feet above.

"A second's rest and I began crawling on my hands and knees, feeling for that which I wanted, yet feared to find. Richley clung to the painter and was flung up with terrible force.

"Of the occupants of this boat only two survived. We found seven more survivors [from the second lifeboat] on the rocks. We nine, Campbell losing a wife and daughter, crept as high up as we could and lay down in a pile for warmth and waited for daylight, while the rain and snow beat down upon us. At daylight we found a way of climbing up the precipitous bluff at whose feet we had been cast.

"Before leaving, however, daylight showed us a poor fellow lying near whose face had been broken in and who had gone insane.

"We pulled him as far as we could but had to abandon him, as he was helpless.

"On the bluff above we fortunately found a rude trail through the brush which seemed to follow a telegraph wire. We reasoned that if we could follow this line far enough, we would come to some habitation and thus tell the world of the plight of the hundred passengers still on the *Valencia*."

Bunker's account omitted any reference to the fact that his party went for shelter and safety after making it ashore, abandoning over 100 people still on the *Valencia*. They all might have been saved had he turned up at the top of the cliff to receive the line fired from the Lyle gun.

Bunker's action to turn left and find a way to "tell the world" came under immediate attack. It was felt that, instead, he should have tried to reach the shore above the ship. At the inquiry, Charles Allison, the old man who was rescued by the *City of Topeka* from one of the last liferafts, asked some very direct questions of Professor Bunker. These were printed in the *Seattle Times*:

"Why did you run away? Why didn't you come back to help us?

"All we wanted was a single man on top of that cliff to catch a line. We had plenty of lines and means of getting them ashore – or at least a chance to, but no one to catch them. We prayed for the sight of a man up there! Just one man to catch the end of a rope and make it fast to a tree! We were so close! And the rock was so lonesome. Even to have looked at us, as I understand some men did at the end, wouldn't have made it seem so bad – to me at least."

Of the two parties that had reached shore, neither seemed to have made a serious attempt to render assistance. The whole crew which found the telegraph wire had walked to Cape Beale, although one could have easily carried the news while the others could at least have tried to reach the steamer. All the men with Bunker had walked to the telegraph hut, causing Allison to ask if they could not have spared a man or two to come to the wreck.

"I know I feel it all keenly now," Allison said, "and the scene is very fresh in my mind, but perhaps Mr. Bunker is emotional, too. He has reason to be and I sympathize with him deeply in his affliction. But he is able to ask questions and so am I. I would like to have his answered and perhaps he can answer mine.

"Why should they all have run away? It wasn't far from where they were to the cliff above us. They could have got up some way, weak as they were. We didn't have smallpox – we were simply drowning, and all we wanted was a rope...."

The Federal Commission later concluded that when Bunker's party decided to turn west, by far the best chance for rescuing the remaining survivors vanished.

As was later revealed at the inquiry, Bunker's lack of action was only one in an incredible series of missed opportunities and poor decisions that doomed passengers and crew. They began with the fact that there had been no proper boat drill on the *Valencia*. Only two boat crews had been instructed in what to do in an emergency. Many officers and crew didn't even know to which lifeboat they had been assigned.

Then there were questions about the effectiveness of the reed-filled life preservers, and the tule lifebelts. These were filled with cattails, a reed that grows almost everywhere along the American northwest coast, and Bunker reported that they had sunk rather than support a person's weight. At the time this story was reported by Bunker, the question was raised that if Government Inspection had allowed bad life preservers and improper conditions in lifeboats on the *Valencia*, were life-saving appliances on all other vessels in the area of Puget Sound just as bad? One of the men conducting the hearing was Inspector of Hulls and Boilers, B. B. Whitney. He rigorously defended the lifebelts, noting:

"The United States regulations allow the use of tule [reed] life preservers under certain conditions, specified in the report of the Supervising Inspector. There are two kinds mentioned that come up to the requirements. One is the Dunant's tule life-preserver, made in California; the other is the Le-Duc tule life-preserver, made in the East. These preservers are inspected at the factories and after they are placed aboard ship. We have a man visit the factory there once a month or oftener. If the preservers do not show the required buoyancy, they are rejected.

Among Bunker's many criticisms was that the life preservers and lifeboats on board were useless, and had failed in the moment of need. He also charged that the examinations of the *Valencia* and her equipment must have been cursory and limited to simply making sure that the proper number of lifebelts and lifeboats were at hand, rather than to inspect their real condition and effectiveness.

It was reported that inspections of passenger steamers at Seattle had been seemingly quite strict and thorough. There even had been some complaints by shipping companies that they had been too thorough, that the companies had to face much trouble and expense. The *Valencia* had been examined and passed by local Inspectors only a short time before the wreck, resulting in another serious accusation – were the Inspectors qualified. This question was asked not by Bunker, but by a "master mariner" who remained anonymous. These charges had a lot of bite, and were directed squarely at the Inspectors who had passed the *Valencia* and her equipment. It was revealed that two or three days before this inspection, an Admiral Kempf had come to the Tacoma area for his own tour of inspection. As a result, 93 out of 120 tule life preservers on Puget Sound work boats had been condemned, and yet they had allowed the *Valencia* and other Pacific Coast Company boats to retain them.

There was an additional serious accusation: The civil service law required Inspectors to have served at least five consecutive years as masters of ocean-going steamships. They were also to have practical knowledge of ship construction before being able to qualify. Inspector Whitney, one of the men conducting the hearing at Seattle, seemed to be woefully short of this kind of experience. In fact Inspector Whitney's first experience on an ocean-going steamer had been when he took the *Centennial* from Seattle to San Francisco on a single voyage, and then had made one voyage to Honolulu. He had then been to Honolulu once more on a freighter. The entire extent of his experience was these three voyages – a total of six months.

Although the Federal Commission made no mention of the controversy surrounding the qualifications of the inspectors, it found that "excepting possibly her bulkheads and one set of davits" the construction and equipment of the *Valencia*, so far as the safety of her passengers was concerned, was excellent.

The Commission did, however, wonder if there might have been a problem with the *Valencia's* bulkheads. The *Valencia* had carried sugar for 15 years, and it was charged that this cargo had honeycombed her bulkheads, thus weakening them and contributing greatly to her quick sinking.

Dr. Malcolm Faziell, a chemist with B.C. Sugar in Vancouver, felt that pure sugar would have had no effect on steel. It was Faziell's opinion, however, that there was one way this could have happened. The *Valencia's* cargo would have been raw sugar. It contains many impurities which by themselves could have been corrosive, especially if the sugar got wet and started to rot.

A number of organic acids like lactic, formic, and acetic now might have been present, as well as ferric acetate and permeate. These acids could have had a destructive effect on the steel bulkheads, and the honeycombing could have been caused by severe subsequent corrosion. But a counterbalance

Frank Connors, left, survived but George Jesse died. Both men were in the rigging when the mast broke. Conners urged Jesse to "Come and take a chance." Jesse replied, "I can't. I've got someone to look after here." He sacrificed his life trying to help others.

to this theory is that rotting sugar has an extremely strong and disagreeable odour.

Dr. Faziell, in fact, stated that "...it would have stunk to high heaven." Nobody ever referred to any strong odour on the *Valencia*, although a thorough cleaning might have removed any traces. The fact remained, however, that the *Valencia* took on water very quickly, and most of her hull was soon destroyed by pounding waves.

The Commission dealt in as much detail as possible with all of these charges. Its report stated that during the year preceding the disaster, the *Valencia's* equipment had been inspected three times, the last taking place only three weeks before the tragedy. As far as could be ascertained from these inspections, her equipment was in excellent condition and in all respects fulfilled the requirements of the law and regulations, with some very minor exceptions. What these were was not spelled out. Her engines and machinery had been in good condition and her hull recently overhauled and repaired but there was no mention if work had been conducted on her bulkheads.

The Commission also addressed the complaints about the buoyancy of the tule life preservers. Statements of witnesses who claimed that these life preservers had weighed between 50 and 60 pounds when they got out of the water were dismissed as incorrect. In the Commission's opinion they must have reflected the exhausted condition of the wearers. The cubic capacity of the lifebelts was checked and it was determined that if filled entirely with water, they could not weigh more than 40 pounds.

To prove this point a public test was made by the Commission. Eight tule life preservers, taken off eight different ships in the harbour at Seattle, were immersed for 17 hours in salt water with a 20-pound weight attached. They were all afloat after the test, the heaviest having absorbed just under 10 pounds of water. Other tests conducted in San Francisco where the life preservers were manufactured had shown that these had supported 34 pounds for short periods, ample to support a person because of the buoyancy of salt water. These tests for all practical purposes put an end to the lifebelt controversy.

CHAPTER SIX

The Abandoned Survivors

Back in Victoria, on Wednesday night, the *Queen City* had reached the outer wharf about six in the evening. She reported that there were still at least 20 to 30 people clinging to the rigging of the *Valencia's* aftermast, with the fore part of the steamer entirely submerged. The only parts of the *Valencia* still above the water when she left the scene were her masts, her smoke stack, and part of the after cabin on the hurricane deck. The steamer was now reported to lay broadside against the shore and at high water, which was expected at 1:30 p.m., the greater part of her hull would have been submerged. According to the *Queen City*, there was a heavy southwest sea rolling in, and the houses left on the aft deck would soon be washed away. The remaining survivors were still frantically signalling and waving from the rigging. To those on the *Queen City* the sight of the people who had tied themselves to the rigging must have been heartbreaking, but they did nothing to help.

Because those on the *Queen City* admitted seeing the survivors, it is difficult to understand why the crew of the Canadian tug boat *Czar* stated otherwise. The *Czar* was a much smaller vessel, and got much closer to the *Valencia* than the *Queen City*. She nevertheless returned and reported that there was no one on board. Since survivors were in the rigging, they must have been seen by those on the *Czar*. Only because the *Czar* was a Canadian vessel was she saved from severe prosecution in the U.S.

Even Captain Cousins of the *Queen City*, after reaching Victoria, charged the *Czar* with cowardice. It was the most devastating accusation that could be made in a situation where lives were at stake. The *Czar* had not only deserted the people clinging to the rigging but also even denied their very existence. Cousins claimed that he went in as close as possible with his ship, against the warnings of his pilot, and "I begged the captain of the *Czar* to go in and try to get a line to her, but he refused, shouting back that he was going to Cape Beale for shelter himself before the storm came up."

But Cousins himself wasn't blameless. He was asked by Bunker why he also ran away, leaving no vessel to look for survivors after the *Valencia* broke up. Cousins stated:

"That is a mistake. I did not leave until ordered to do so by the assistant superintendent of the company, Mr. Pharo, who came up in the *City of Topeka* and ordered me to proceed to Victoria, the *City of Topeka* meanwhile relieving us. There was a fearful sea running at the time we were off the wreck and I would not allow a boat to be lowered. [This statement was not in accordance with later testimony of people ashore. They thought that a small boat could have got out from the steamer with little problem. Indeed, there was strong evidence of a break in the surf just in front of the *Valencia*, possibly caused by leaking oil. This gap was reported to be about 50 feet wide and would have allowed easy access to the steamer.]

"We discovered the wreck by accident as we were skirting the shore," Cousins continued. "The weather was so nasty and boisterous that one could see the shore only at intervals. It was 9:00 o'clock Wednesday morning when we sighted the wreck. At 9:30 the *Salvor* and *Czar* came up, and I whistled for them to stop, but they said that the wreck was six miles further on and it was sometime before I could get them to stop.

"The *Czar* finally sheered in a little ways and came back reporting that the entire hull was under water and there was no living person on board. At that time I was within three-quarters of a mile of the wreck and could plainly see people on board.

"I tried to get the *Czar* to go in and get near enough to fire a line to the wreck, but she refused. She was the only craft there that could have accomplished anything...."

Two passengers who were on the *Queen City* when she left for the wreck, P. C. Jorgenson and D. C. Sullivan who were chief boatswain's mates in the navy, had been put in charge of 40 seamen. They later blamed the people on the vessel for having made no effort at all to reach the wreck. They were under the impression, and stated as such, that a boat could have easily reached the grounded steamer.

The *Salvor* apparently had no direct contact with the *Queen City*, and received her information from the *Czar,* whatever that might have been. In any case, the tragic result

In contrast to those on land and shore who refused to help the survivors on the *Valencia* was the action of Captain E. Gillam of the *Princess Maquinna*. On November 23, 1915, the sailing ship *Carelmapu*, below, was badly damaged in a storm near Barkley Sound. Captain Gillam, despite a gale with seas so rough that he was debating whether or not to return to Tofino, without hesitation went to the aid of the storm-battered *Carelmapu*. He pumped oil to help lessen the mountainous seas and dropped both of his anchors, intending to back towards the sailing ship. But a huge wave struck the *Princess Maquinna*, tearing the anchor winch out of the steel deck. His own ship now in peril, Captain Gillam had to hacksaw his anchor cables and leave. A few hours later another wave washed the sailing ship onto the reefs. Of 24 seamen on board, only five and the ship's dog survived.

was that all these ships departed, leaving those still alive on the *Valencia* to face an empty horizon.

It was clear from earlier testimony that the last survivors were not totally alone, although their fate was already sealed. On the cliffs above them three men watched the final, horrifying scene. As mentioned earlier, they were P. C. Daykin, son of the lighthouse keeper at Carmanah Light, the lineman Logan, and a trapper named Martin. When reading their testimony at the Seattle hearing, it is hard to conceal feelings of anger and frustration at so much incompetence and lack of compassion.

All three men concurred in their opinion that lifeboats could have reached the steamer quite easily at this time. There was a gap in the breakers in front of the vessel, and the seas had calmed down considerably. They had also witnessed the last raft leaving, which was later picked up by the *City of Topeka*.

At the investigation, Daykin explained what happened when the *Valencia* finally broke up, folded in the middle, and spilled the last survivors into the sea.

Q. Could you see which way the bodies went?

A. No.

Q. The people sank immediately when they went into the water?

A. No, they all had something to hang onto.

Q. Did they go to seaward, too, on this wreckage?

A. Quite a number were drowned right there.

Q. How many would you say went out on wreckage?

A. I couldn't say.

Q. How far out could you see them on the wreckage?

A. There was one piece about ten feet square with four people on it about a quarter of a mile outside the breakers.

Q. And that went outside the breakers?

A. Yes.

Q. And then went westward?

A. Yes.

Q. Did you see it capsize?

A. No.

Q. When you last saw it they were still floating?

A. Yes.

Q. Did you see any other wreckage with people on it go out to sea?

A. Yes.

Q. About how many could you see?

A. I couldn't tell; made no attempt to count them.

Q. When you last saw them they were still floating?

A. Yes.

Q. Seaward?

A. Yes.

By this time there were no ships left to pull them out of the frigid waters. When asked if the people in the water had life preservers on, Daykin answered: "Everybody I saw I think had life preservers on; as far as I could see they all had life preservers. Some of them didn't get away from the ship."

Q. Could you say about how many were left in the rigging when you left the scene of the wreck?

A. There was 25 on one side, and maybe as many on the other, and maybe more.

Q. They were in the rigging?

A. Yes.

The Commission must have been stunned by the testimony of these three. According to their testimony about 75 to 80 people were still seen huddled under blankets and hanging in the rigging. When they left more than half had been spilled into the sea. When asked how many were still afloat when they left Daykin's answer was: "I couldn't tell."

Q. They were scattered all around there in the water?

A. Yes.

Q. Going to seaward and to the westward?

A. Yes.

Q. Did the life preservers buoy them up when they didn't have any wreckage?

A. Seemed to as far as I could tell.

From the testimony given at the hearing by Martin: "... those on the west side of the mast were very still; there were one or two men bidding these people goodbye as they went out to sea."

Q. How do you know that?

A. They were waving their hands.

The investigators listened to Daykin's testimony with what must have been pain and disbelief. As stated during the inquiry, Daykin, Logan and Martin left Carmanah sometime Tuesday afternoon and walked as far as the Clanewah [Klanawa] River where they spent the night. They crossed the river at about half past nine Wednesday morning, almost two hours after first light. Why so late? We will never know.

On their way to the wreck, which according to Daykin they reached "about noon," they took time out for tea at "The Indian Ranch." Why then, being on their way to where people were at the mercy of the sea, would they stop for tea? Did they not feel the urgency of the situation? Surely they knew of the hopeless situation on board. At this time, although it is hard to say with certainty, chances were that the line fired to shore that morning still lay limp across the top of the cliff, just waiting to be picked up by someone.

Inspectors Whitney and Turner apparently could not believe what they were hearing. They asked at one point if the party had not maybe considered this whole trip a mere picnic. Later, however, a different story emerged about the late arrival of the shore party, although this account was never confirmed by any of the three men.

A cable operator named Jennings from Bamfield stated that the delay was the fault of the Nitinat Indians, that they were responsible for Daykin, Logan, and Martin not reaching the wreck at sundown Tuesday. Why and how he came to make this statement is not known. But Jennings claimed that after arriving at Nitinat Creek – actually a tidal gap of 300 to 500 feet at the entrance to Nitinat Lake – the three men asked the Indians to ferry them across the swollen creek. The Indians demanded a payment of $4 a head. The men had no money and could not persuade the Indians to get them across. Because of this delay they did not reach the opposite shore until late that night and were forced to wait until the following morning.

When Logan was later asked by the Inspectors if he did not think that arriving at the scene as early as possible should have been their first concern, he stated that he was not sure exactly what they could have done to save the people still on board, but admitted that at least they would have had five more hours to try.

The three men finally arrived on top of the bluff and, following the broken Lyle gun line which was still lying across the trail, came to the point overlooking the wreck. The *Valencia* was by now partially submerged only 15 to 20 yards from shore. Now their action, or lack of it, became puzzling. Could they not have tried to throw a line to the ship, using a stone for weight? Even if their line looked too short, could they not have tied the end of the broken Lyle gun line to it and at least tried to reach the ship?

They had also brought 100 feet of line with them. Why did they not try and scale downward onto the rocks, establishing some contact with the stern of the ship? Maybe the remaining passengers could have drifted a line towards them to connect with the line on shore.

But try they did not. Below them huddled many survivors, their eyes looking up at the men on top of the cliff. With them now lay their only hope. When they arrived, the people on board had cheered wildly. Some shrieked in fear and distress, their voices plainly audible through the roaring surf. But their last hope on the quickly dying ship was soon crushed when no help was forthcoming from the men on the cliff. Incredibly, the shore party did not even stay till the end.

They saw one giant roller sweep in. The starboard side broke away, carrying those clinging to the rigging into the sea. Then the funnel stays were carried away and the funnel fell. Finally, the poop deck broke in the centre and enclosed the unfortunate victims. Elsewhere, bodies littered the sea, a few survivors among them. The men on the cliff walked away shortly after a final wave broke the steamer into pieces, with human forms still fighting bravely for their lives in the cold water.

CHAPTER SEVEN

Most Shameful Incident in Canadian Maritime History

Alarming news of Indians who had begun robbing the victims they found on the rocks appeared in the local papers. Quickly, arrangements were made in Victoria to receive the bodies and a temporary morgue was set up in freight sheds on the harbour front. All bodies were required to be brought to Victoria, where an immigration officer took charge of them and their possessions. The U.S. Revenue Cutter *Grant* had taken some bodies directly to Seattle, but was no longer permitted to do so. Bunker and his party, as well as Daykin, Logan and Martin, were trying to collect and identify the scores of bodies.

A major problem was that removing the bodies by land was simply impossible. Access to shore in many places was blocked by cliffs, while travel through the thick bush was hopeless. It was decided that the only possible way was bringing the bodies to waiting vessels by boats. Soon it was realized that the seaworthy Indian canoes were the most suitable vessels for this task of challenging the surf. The Indians consequently played a major role in bringing out the victims.

Other vital assistance was provided by the tug *Lorne* under command of Captain Butler. She had originally been sent by the Mayor of Victoria, who was also on board, carrying a surf boat and naval crew, as well as medical personnel and supplies. Although she arrived too late to help during the greatest need, she was instrumental in recovering many bodies. A description of them was printed in the newspapers to aid identification by relatives or friends:

"Male – Taken from beach near wreck, 5 feet; age about 16, weight about 110; dark hair; dark clothes, square cut coat with faint light stripes; brown ribbed underclothing; brown socks; limbs heavy for boy, wore two rings on little finger.

The tug *Lorne*, carrying medical personnel and supplies, arrived too late but helped recover many bodies. Indian canoes, however, proved the most suitable craft to challenge the surf. The ones below, carved from huge cedar trees, are carrying a wedding party.

Female – Taken from beach near wreck, height 5 feet, 2 inches; weight about 150 pounds; features unrecognizable, part of skull gone, badly decomposed.

By February 6 there remained little hope of picking up any more recognizable bodies. Many of the victims finally reached their homes and were buried by family and friends, but many more lie in shallow and often unmarked graves along the shore, and many were never found.

On February 3 a crude wooden cross was erected somewhere on Long Beach, marking the grave of the first unknown victim. There would be others. Decomposition of the bodies soon made it impossible to send them home.

But even as the bodies were being recovered, the first exploration of the wreck began. An eyewitness recalled floating over it in a small boat. The *Valencia's* hull was plainly visible, her plates broken, as was the pilothouse. A floating spar protruded about seven feet out of the sea, and the tops of her boilers, cylinders and safety valves were easily recognizable in the clear water. Soon after, her boilers disappeared. It was rumoured that the *Salvor* or the *Czar* had salvaged them, leaving in many people a feeling of disgust.

Several investigations ensued over the months following the sinking. They ranged from the major U.S. one already mentioned to others investigating navigational hazards in Juan de Fuca Strait, hoping to make the Graveyard of the Pacific safer for navigators.

There were, however, serious charges as to the impartiality of the investigating bodies, with special reference to Inspectors Whitney and Turner in Seattle. The *Seattle Star* made caustic comments which cast serious doubt on the final conclusions reached:

"Victor H. Metcalf, the Secretary of the Department of Commerce and Labor in President Roosevelt's cabinet, owes his appointment to Senator George C. Perkins of California, who in turn is closely associated with the Pacific Coast Steamship Company, owners of the wrecked *Valencia*. Senator Piles, one of the men with whom Mr. Metcalf should keep on the most friendly terms, is the Seattle attorney for the Pacific Steamship Company."

The paper continued to say that Inspectors Whitney and Turner had been direct appointees of Victor Metcalf. As these

Inspectors were to investigate the cause of the disaster, and to assess any blame on the Pacific Coast Steamship Company, it was assumed that they had given the company a much better treatment by the scope of their questions than it deserved. The paper noted that they had discouraged any further charges in regards to the poor quality of the life preservers and the condition of the lifeboats.

In fairness, however, it should be mentioned that Senator Piles had been working hard only weeks before the *Valencia* disaster to have a new life-saving station established at Cape Flattery.

He had introduced a bill on December 7, 1905, into the Upper House of Congress which read: "Be it enacted ... that the Secretary of the Treasury is hereby authorized to establish a life-saving station in the vicinity of Cape Flattery or Flattery Rocks, on the coast of Washington, at such point as the general superintendent of the life-saving service may recommend."

The Secretary of the Treasury also wrote a strong letter endorsing the bill and urging its immediate passage.

On the Canadian side, the Victoria Board of Trade, led by president T. W. Paterson, held a meeting soon after the wreck. A special committee was appointed to make recommendations to Ottawa. The meeting unanimously endorsed a resolution demanding immediate improvements on the west coast. They also adopted similar conclusions reached at a citizens' meeting which had been referred to the Department of Marine and Fisheries in Ottawa. The Victoria Board of Trade also referred these findings to its own Harbour and Navigation Committee to more thoroughly investigate the requirements for the greater safety of life and ships on that portion of the coast.

The main question was the prevention of further wrecks and the need of greater life-saving measures on the west coast of Vancouver Island. From the discussion emerged three principal causes of disasters – heavy gales and thick weather; a strong current to the northwest along the western coast of Washington State and Vancouver Island; and fog banks in late fall and early winter that lie along the coastline of both Mainland and Island, while beyond is clear weather.

It was suggested that the treacherous northerly current should be more emphasized on charts, and somehow brought to the notice of mariners not familiar with the Strait of Juan de

Fuca. The fog banks were another little known local hazard, and put ships in great danger of running ashore. One suggestion was that a vessel be provided to cruise off Cape Flattery. It could be a schooner with auxiliary power – a lightship at sea – to orient vessels before they entered the fog banks.

This suggestion, however, was not accepted by the other members. It was felt that it would be of little use as the mariners would not know the ship's location. But it was thought possible that life-saving could be effectively accomplished from the sea even in stormy weather by equipping vessels with long ropes by which lifeboats which were drifted onto an endangered vessel could be drawn back to the ships rendering help.

There also was yet another mention of the poor quality of inspections. One member, C. H. Lugrin, stated that he was aware from his own personal knowledge that the inspections of sea-going steamers of American registry were perfunctory. The result was other deplorable incidents, reinforcing the previously heard accusations against the Inspectors of Hulls and Boilers, Whitney and Turner.

Everyone agreed, however, and told the Dominion Government that the coast needed new lights and powerful fog signals, together with a perfect telegraph and telephone service to keep vessels off the rocks along Vancouver Island's west coast. The trail along the telegraph wires should be cleared, roads built to allow moving of life-saving equipment, and a number of shelter huts constructed at convenient points. Each hut should be stocked with provisions to sustain shipwrecked mariners until help could be summoned by telegraph.

The public argument of the pros and cons of wireless telegraph services and their benefit to shipping in this area resulted in a number of comments. Strangely enough, the benefits of such a system was challenged by Captain J. W. Troup, the General Superintendent of the Canadian Pacific Railway's B.C. Coast Service.

A different opinion was voiced in a letter to the *Daily Colonist*. It identified many of the problems west coast residents felt they had in getting money from the Dominion Government in Ottawa to improve navigation:

"Sir — In reading the various letters touching on the recent appalling wreck of the *Valencia* on the west coast, I have been somewhat surprised that among the many suggestions put forth to avert future similar catastrophes, not once has the practicality of wireless telegraphy been mentioned, although the utility of the same has been so recently demonstrated on the Atlantic shore, both as a life and property saver, which the following will show: Not later than the 10th ult. a frightful storm threatened to destroy the lightship anchored on Nantucket Shoal for the protection of trans-Atlantic steamers; the vessel having sprung a leak, the pumps were found to be inadequate to cope with the inrush of water and the following day a wireless call was sent forth for help, which was immediately responded to and assistance sent out from three different points, one of the rescuing boats taking the lightship in tow, and being finally forced to transfer the crew, only in time, however, as the lightship sank ten minutes later.

"Another case in which a calamity was probably averted through this medium is that of the *S.S. York*. She was warned on the 20th ult. by a wireless message from the American liner *Philadelphia* to alter her course to avoid a large iceberg directly in her charted path off the Grand Banks. Had the *Valencia* had wireless apparatus on her (which should be made compulsory on all passenger steamers), and were stations erected along our dangerous west coast, this disaster might have been prevented.

"It seems rather peculiar that the Dominion Government has turned all her attention in this line to the East Coast, having already made contracts with the Marconi Wireless Company for the erection of twenty-three stations (twenty of which are now operating) along the coast of Labrador and Gulf of St. Lawrence, which according to the report of the late Minister of Marine and Fisheries, the Hon. R. Prefontaine, were giving complete satisfaction, whilst our shores, which are proving equally dangerous, are left unprotected.

"The suggestion of one of your correspondents that signal telegraph stations be placed every ten miles or so in order that assistance may be speedily got in case of wrecks is not all that is necessary; what we require is a preventative, which, I think, would be found in wireless telegraphy. The matter could not be more forcefully brought to the attention of the Dominion Government than at the present moment, when so many homes are mourning the loss of loved ones who perished within sight of land. Hoping that this suggestion may not be altogether lost, and thanking you for permitting me to encroach on your valuable space,

"signed Pro Bono Publico."

People on the American side were equally appalled. The establishment of wireless stations on shore and aboard ship and on ocean-going tugs in the area of Cape Flattery equipped with proper life-saving apparatus had long been requested, but never put into action. Some 200 wrecks and deaths of 1,500 people in the area should have been more than enough incentive. W. E. Pearce, General Manager of the Pacific Coast Steamship Company, charged: "I say the government is to blame! If our senators had any gumption about them, we would have had an ocean-going tug, properly equipped, up in the vicinity of the *Valencia* wreck months ago! There hasn't been as much preparation up around Vancouver Island, the most dangerous 100 miles of coast on this side of the continent, to save lives as there has been in five miles of coast on the north of England!"

As the complete story of the wreck unfolded, Pearce was furious: "I simply believed at the time that no aid on earth could reach those people. But with the true story of the wreck at hand, had the proper life-saving apparatus been provided by the government, not a man, woman or child would have been lost!"

On February 7, 1906, the President of the United States issued the following order to the Secretary of Commerce and Labor:

"Sir: You are hereby directed to instruct Lawrence 0. Murray, Assistant Secretary of Commerce and Labor, and Herbert Knox Smith, Deputy Commissioner of Corporations, as well as Captain William T. Burwell, U.S. Navy, who will ... proceed to Seattle, Washington, and there to make thorough and complete investigation of all the circumstances attending the wreck of the steamer *Valencia* and the cause or causes thereof, and any misconduct, negligence, or dereliction of duty on the part on anyone related thereto and having any bearing upon the loss of life occasioned by said disaster; and also, as you may direct, to investigate such other matters bearing upon the safety of traffic in navigable waters of the United States in that vicinity with recommendations for such departmental or legislative action as may be indicated by said report and findings.

"Very truly, yours,   Theodore Roosevelt"

In accordance with this request, the Federal Commission of Investigation was formed the same day. The first report ordered by President Roosevelt was published only two months later. It was the best account of what took place. The conclusions of the Federal Commission were detailed and showed surprising accuracy and insight.

Basically, the Commission came to the opinion that the *Valencia* went ashore through the faulty navigation of Captain Johnson, her master. He had not required a boat drill of his crew. Half of the crew of the *Valencia* had been new men, and the Commission felt that the omission by the Captain of having a proper boat drill before the commencement of the voyage nullified to a large extent the usefulness of the boat equipment on board.

The Commission also acknowledged that Captain Johnson's conduct after the vessel struck and the boats had been lowered was satisfactory, and that he apparently did all he could for the safety and comfort of his passengers, and showed courage and good judgement.

The Commission also dealt with the look-out posted in the bow of the ship. As he was one of the victims, his testimony could not be heard. It seemed remarkable to the investigators and certainly peculiar that this man, a full 100 feet in front of the bridge, should not have seen the rocks and cliffs first. Why did he not signal the bridge? The look-out had been on duty since 6 p.m. Monday, a full six hours when the vessel struck. The Commission thought that even a good sailor could not keep an effective look-out during foul weather for this length of time. They concluded that this watch system, a responsibility of the Captain as well, was responsible for the fact that land was not reported by the look-out at all.

As far as the life preservers were concerned, the Commission felt that as they had been allowed by regulation, it was up to the Federal Government to further investigate the buoyant qualities of the tule lifebelts, but found no blame should be attributed to the steamship company for having them on board. Captain Cousins, master of the *Queen City*, was criticized for not picking up any available seagoing tug on his way

Pachena Lighthouse, built as a result of the *Valencia* disaster, and Tofino's first rescue lifeboat

to the wreck in the vicinity of Neah Bay. The tugs were there at that time, and so was the *Queen City*. She cruised the waters all through the night until daylight Wednesday morning and certainly had the opportunity to do so.

It was felt that the order given to Captain Cousins to leave the site of the wreck and to return to Victoria was wrong, and the Commission found both Mr. Pharo of the Pacific Coast Steamship Company and Captain Patterson of the *City of Topeka* highly censurable for having issued and sanctioned this order. The Commission found it hard to understand this command, and thought that in all probability it had been the desire by the company that the *Queen City* should return and resume her regular business in the commercial interests of the company.

The report also stated, however, that the Pacific Coast Steamship Company, throughout the entire matter, seemed to have spared no effort nor expense to effect rescue and to relieve the survivors, except in this one case. The Commission concluded that there had been need at the wreck for "as many vessels as could be gotten." It outright dismissed the argument that the *City of Topeka* was to take over from the *Queen City*, and therefore the *Queen City's* presence was no longer required.

The findings further noted that the officers on the *City of Topeka* never saw the wreck, and therefore could take no means of rescue. The officers of the *Queen City*, however, had been in sight of the wreck for about one hour. The question of sending boats to the wreck was apparently discussed by the officers on the *Queen City*, but unanimously decided against. This failure to even attempt sending a boat to the wreck or drifting a raft to it, or to fire a line across it, raised questions that the Commission was unable to understand or answer.

The Commission admitted that unquestionably the men on the *Queen City*, as a matter of common humanity, must be assumed to have tried to do the best they could under the circumstances. And yet there seemed to have been a good chance of establishing some contact with the wreck, either by way of using boats, or by drifting rafts to her, which was not realized. There was no doubt that ordinary lifeboats could have been safely taken toward the wreck as long as they kept outside of the line of breakers, which was about 100 to 200 yards from the bow of the *Valencia*. If the *Queen City* and the *City of Topeka* had remained near the wreck, and had seamen been standing by in the boats in this location, many of the survivors which were drifting seaward could have been picked up and saved.

Once so close to the ship, the men in the boats might very well have discovered that they could approach the wreck, maybe through the reported oil slick just off the bow. The excuse from the *Queen City* that in her opinion no boats could be launched was disproved a short while later when the *City of Topeka* launched such a boat to pick up the survivors in the raft.

The Commission stated that there certainly had been no display of heroic daring that day that had so often marked other emergencies at sea in the past. This statement brought no honour to the captains of the *Queen City* or the *City of Topeka*.

The Commission was reluctant to voice any opinion on the conduct of the *Salvor* and the *Czar*, these being vessels of Canadian registry, and their officers not being subject to American Law.

The most important conclusion by the Commission was saved until last, and was that "...the primary and greatest cause of the loss of life was the defective state of the aids to navigation and preservation of life in the shape of lighthouses, fog signals, life-saving equipment, and means of communication in the vicinity of the wreck."

The Coroner's inquest held in Victoria, and a Dominion Government investigation headed by Captain Gaudin, did not answer any more of the questions raised. The fact was recognized, however, that from the evidence submitted Captain Christenson of the *Czar* had sufficient information to at least raise doubt in his mind as to whether there was life on board the *Valencia*. It must be assumed that he saw the people clinging to the rigging, and huddling on deck, as he was so much closer to her than even the *Queen City*, from which the people on the *Valencia* had been clearly visible. The conclusion was that the *Czar* had run away for shelter in one of the most shameful incidents in Canadian maritime history.

The Thirty-Ninth Annual Report of the Department of Marine and Fisheries in Ottawa was presented in April 1907 by the Minister, L. P. Brodeur, who had long neglected conditions out west. The report mentioned the existence of 98 life-saving stations in the Dominion of Canada, none in British Columbia.

There was, however, some movement. The most visible was the construction of Pachena Point Lighthouse in 1907. The report stated that the first steps had also been taken towards the inauguration of a life-saving service. Construction had begun in Vancouver on a self-righting, self-bailing boat 35 feet long. Also, a crew for this boat was being organized and trained in Vancouver. The report didn't say how one boat could serve some 6,000 miles that B.C's mountainous coastline presented to mariners.

It was also mentioned that the Department was considering establishing a life-saving station at Bamfield Creek, with quarters for the crew, and also at Clo-oose, Ucluelet, and Clayoquet Sound. It was also suggested that a lifeboat should be placed on board the *Salvor.*

Strangely enough, there is no surviving copy of the Commission of Enquiry held by the Canadian Government on February 5, 1906, in Victoria. Apparently the Commission's findings and recommendations were in the hands of the Minister, Louis Brodeur, from where they never resurfaced.

On March 19, 1906, the Official Report of the Debates of the House of Commons include a direct question to the Minister in regards to the wrecks on the Pacific Coast. MP Ralph Smith wanted to know exactly how many wrecks had occurred, how many lives and how much cargo had been lost, and was the Government doing anything?

Brodeur answered evasively that the information requested was now being prepared, and would be available at a later time. In the Fourth Session of the Tenth Parliament held between November 1907 and January 1908, Brodeur stated that five wireless telegraph stations were under construction on the Pacific Coast, but made no mention of whether any of these were being built on the west coast of Vancouver Island.

The Report on the Debates also mentioned the Bamfield Creek lifeboat. Asked about the cost and date of purchase of this lifeboat, Minister Brodeur answered that the boat had been delivered on November 7, 1907, at a cost of $10,900. It was now a full two years after the *Valencia* disaster. Another point of argument which was brought up in Parliament was the fact that this boat had been purchased in the United States, although there were a number of Canadian boat builders who could have built lifeboats of the same quality. But they were not even given an opportunity.

Brodeur simply stated that there had not been sufficient time to look for a builder in Canada, but "if any further lifeboats are required, [we] will, if practicable, have them built in Canada."

The second very tangible result of the *Valencia* tragedy was the construction of the West Coast Trail, which was completed in 1908.

On the stretch between Bamfield and Shelter Bight, where the *Valencia* went down, the Trail was 12 feet wide, making it possible to move equipment by horse-drawn carriage. For the remaining distance to Carmanah Point it was only four feet wide because the terrain was much more difficult. In all, the trail required 62 culverts and 21 bridges. The work was accomplished using picks and shovels, the only piece of "equipment" a horse-drawn scraper which moved ahead of the men as they cleared the torn out roots and trees.

(Today the trail has been rebuilt and as part of Pacific Rim National Park attracts thousands of hikers each year. So many, in fact, that there is now a reservation system.)

As noted, the Canadian inquest held in Victoria in 1906 did not uncover anything new. The *Valencia* affair was laid to rest. No disciplinary action resulted either in the U.S. or in Canada.

CHAPTER EIGHT

Myth of the Ghost Ship and Lifeboat No. 5

In the years following the disaster, there were several stories about a "ghost ship" and other unexplainable occurrences and findings. Seafaring people have been superstitious through the centuries, and it was only natural that a tragedy like this one would have its effect on popular lore in the area.

For example, five months after the disaster an Indian fisherman, Clanewah Tom, and his wife were paddling along the beaches adjacent to Shelter Bight when they were attracted by the gaping mouth of a sea cave. Curious, Tom swam inside, but came back quickly, pale and out of breath. He later reported that he had seen a lifeboat inside the cave. It was still afloat, and contained eight skeletons.

Carmanah lightkeeper W. P. Daykin heard about it, and dispatched his two sons to investigate. The lighthouse tender *Quadra* got up steam, and also attempted to locate the mysterious lifeboat. But the searchers could not enter the cavern as the relentless surf would have pounded them to death. They decided that Tom must have visited the cave during an extremely low tide. His report of the skeleton-manned lifeboat remains unsolved.

One other discovery, however, was very true – at least in some respects – and that was the discovery of the *Valencia's* lifeboat No. 5. According to Second Officer Petterson, this was the first boat to leave the ship late Monday night. Her passengers were spilled into the sea and drowned when the davits broke. Boatswain Tim McCarthy, however, claims to have left the *Valencia* Tuesday morning on No. 5. Be that as it may, enticed by the mention in several books of the discovery of this lifeboat in Barkley Sound 25 years after the wreck, I did some research.

I discovered that the name plate of lifeboat No. 5 was in the British Columbia Maritime Museum in Victoria. I called Director and Curator John MacFarlane for information about where the rest of the boat might be. His interest aroused, John talked to his father about this incident, which in turn sparked discussion among the old-time seafarers in Victoria to see if they knew anything.

I visited the Maritime Museum in Victoria to see and "feel" the nameplate of the lifeboat, the only tangible reminder of the *Valencia*. The name plate is displayed on the second floor, together with a drawing of the lighthouse at Pachena Point, and a picture of Minnie Paterson and her husband and children at Cape Beale.

The ragged piece of galvanized metal was protected behind plexiglass, the name *Valencia* clearly visible in a dark grey colour. I asked John if the plexiglass could be removed, as it would reflect the flash on my camera. But I also had another motive: I wanted to touch this piece, perhaps experience a spiritual connection with the people who had so tragically lost their lives nearly a century ago. John agreed to remove the protective cover and we walked towards his office. After we sat down he told me the following story:

John's father was about eight or nine years old, living with his family on the Victoria waterfront. He loved boats, and always kept a skiff of some sort tied to a tree near the water. Sometimes he would buy an old lifeboat from ships being wrecked at the shipyard, sometimes he would find one. And quite often he would sell one for pocket money. Sometimes he would row 15 or more hours to bring a boat home. He was just a small boy, and many of the boats he got had been designed to be rowed by eight adult men. In any case, John's father was a pretty lucky lad as his father, Captain George MacFarlane, was a tugboat captain. He towed logs out of Nitinat Lake, mostly, and often brought home a boat he found. This time his son was to be disappointed.

Captain MacFarlane had found a lifeboat adrift in Barkley Sound. As usual, he went over to investigate since there could have been people on board. As he got closer he was able to read the name *Valencia* No. 5. He was puzzled. Mariners more than most other people have a very keen sense of history, and the tragic wreck of the *Valencia*, although it had occurred almost

The survey ship *Quadra* was sent to examine the cave which reportedly contained a lifeboat and eight skeletons.

In the Maritime Museum at Victoria is the name plate from the *Valencia's* No. 5 lifeboat.

25 years earlier, was still much talked about. In Barkley Sound there had been reports of a ghost-ship which resembled the ill-fated steamer, and the Captain wanted some proof that he had really found one of the *Valencia's* lifeboats. Although many sources stated that the lifeboat's paint was in perfect condition, it wasn't. The story in MacFarlane's family is that it was "quite rough and cruddy." The report of the perfect paint was most likely tied to the ghost-ship story to make its discovery seem even stranger than it really was.

As the lifeboat was quite large and heavy, Captain MacFarlane decided not to tow it home. Instead, he brought it to a farmer's field near the inlet to Alberni Canal and beached it.

He then walked up to the farmer's house to borrow an axe to chop off the name plate as proof of his discovery. The farmer agreed, and Captain MacFarlane went to work. It was a tough boat which ruined the farmer's axe, but MacFarlane finally succeeded and took the name plate home. The discovery of the name plate made the news, and was considered sensational.

For the next 25 years it was left in Captain MacFarlane's shed and almost forgotten. In 1955 the British Columbia Maritime Museum opened its doors, and the Captain's wife suddenly remembered the name plate. She finally found it in a corner of their garage. She donated it to the museum but even so no one would see it for over 30 years.

In 1987, John MacFarlane accidentally came across it. After checking, John realized that his family's history had been strangely connected to the *Valencia* for many years. He placed the name plate on exhibition next to a picture of Pachena Point Lighthouse, built as a direct result of the *Valencia* tragedy.

It seems likely that the lifeboat was initially washed up in a storm during high tide, and got stuck in a crevice somewhere in Barkley Sound. Another storm in the early 1930s must have dislodged it from its resting place, and it was washed out to sea where John's grandfather found it. The lifeboat was never seen again.

When John finished his story I had time to go back to re-examine the name plate.

I was alone in the room, looking at the old piece of galvanized steel. I put my hand on the name plate and closed my eyes. I had almost expected some tingling sensation, and a pic-

Indomitable Joe Cigalos, at left in the stern, accompanying a party heading for shore to look for bodies.

ture flashing before my mind of the lifeboat and the people from the *Valencia*. But there was no tingling. Yet I had never felt closer to the *Valencia* and her unlucky passengers. I tried to imagine was it must have been like that dark and stormy night. Although there was nothing I could do to change what happened, I felt sorry and ashamed.

CHAPTER NINE

The Graves

The *Valencia's* grave was visited by divers for many years until the site came under the protection of Pacific Rim National Park. Now access is strictly regulated and the pilfering of valuable artifacts has finally stopped.

In 1986, the Marine Archaeology Unit of Environment Canada began a project to record and inventory the many wrecks in the Graveyard of the Pacific. Prominent wrecks were visited and photographed to record their condition. The depth on the *Valencia's* resting place ranges from 10 feet at the stern, which is almost jammed against the shore, to about 25 feet at the bow. Her bow stands upright on a bed of sand and between two large rocks, pointing seaward, and is relatively intact after almost 100 years in the restless and shallow waters.

Most of the ship's lines can no longer be determined, and all that remains now are the iron plates of her hull. Her propeller shaft and tail shaft are clearly visible, but the engines have broken apart, the immense pistons and cylinders lie crusted on the ocean floor. Next lie the crankshaft and the connecting rods, and off to the side one of her anchors. No blame can be laid on the once proud ship. She had performed faithfully for as long as she could. Even after she crashed ashore, she fought the massive breakers which began sweeping over her, striving to provide desperately needed time for rescuers to save the terrified men, women, and children on board.

A fundamental error in navigation killed her pulse. But that error didn't have to have such fatal consequences. Had people on ships and on land offered so badly needed assistance and tried a little harder, most on board could have survived. In a strange and tragic turn of events, Captain Johnson, so guilty for letting the ship run aground, upheld the tradition of the sea. He stayed with his passengers and his ship and died with them. His action contrasted so sharply with that of many others who could have helped but did nothing.

Walter Raymond, top left, was the last person to leave the *Valencia* and survive. Another lucky person was cook Sam Hancock, above, survivor of four shipwrecks, who had a premonition of disaster when the *Valencia* left San Francisco.

Third officer James Cameron, bottom left, was among those who died. George Long, who went mad on Turrett Island, being supported by two rescuers.

The unwritten law of the sea requires everyone to render whatever assistance necessary to those shipwrecked. This is a matter of honour, of common human decency. Sadly and incomprehensively, these feelings were strangely absent from the minds of many during the *Valencia's* plight. Those cherished values apparently had no meaning to the shore parties, the captains, the business managers and the bureaucrats.

Although the graves of the victims have largely disappeared, a legacy remains – all were betrayed so mercilessly by those who could have helped. For those fateful 40 hours while the *Valencia* was being pounded to pieces beneath 80 or so terrified, desperate human beings, even God must have looked the other way.

BIBLIOGRAPHY

Graham, Donald: *Keepers of the Light*, Harbour Publishing Ltd., 1985.

McKelvie, B.A.: *The Vancouver Province.*

Paterson, T. W.: *British Columbia Shipwrecks*, Stagecoach Publishing Co. Ltd., 1976.

Scott, Bruce R.: *"Breakers Ahead!"* Fleming Review Printing Ltd., 1970.

Transcript of Hearing held before local Inspectors Bion B. Whitney and Robert A. Turner, Seattle, 27 January 1906, U.S. Government Printing Office, Washington. 1906.

Report to The President of The Federal Commission of Investigation, U.S. Government Printing Office, Washington, 1906.

Coroner's Inquest held the 2nd, 3rd, 5th and 6th day of February 1906 in Victoria, B.C.

The *Daily Colonist*, January 24, 25, 26, 28, 30, 31, 1906; February 1, 3, 4, 1906; October 4th, 1936.

The *Seattle Times Daily*, January 23, 24, 25, 26, 27, 28, 1906; February 2, 5, 6, 1906.

Department of Marine and Fisheries, Thirty-Ninth Annual Report, 1906, Ottawa, Fortieth Annual Report, 1907, Ottawa; Forty-First Annual Report, 1908, Ottawa.

INDEX